WHEN I WAS YOUR AGE

Brendan T Finucane

ISBN: 978-1-4834-9338-1 (sc)
ISBN: 978-1-4834-9337-4 (e)

Lulu Publishing Services rev. date: 12/17/2018

DEDICATION

A draft version of this book was written by me in 1989 in honor of our parents' 50th wedding anniversary but was not published. This revised version was written this year (2018), to honor our mother, Patricia T Finucane, who celebrates her 100th birthday on November 17th, 2018.

PREFACE

The inspiration for writing the original book arose when we were preparing to celebrate our parents' 50th wedding anniversary which took place in Roxboro House in the summer of 1989. My family and I were in the process of relocating to Edmonton, Alberta from Atlanta, Georgia. I thought it would be a great idea to write down some of our recollections of growing up in Beechville and share that information with my parents on their 50th anniversary. I made many promises to add to my first efforts but never really got around to doing so until now.

One of the things we have always been fascinated about in our family has been our heritage. We used to quiz my father about how many siblings he had and we never did actually get a full answer to that question in his lifetime. Our dad would start naming siblings and after listing 5 or 6 he would get stuck. There was a very simple explanation for his apparent memory lapse. He was the youngest child in his family and there was a 15 year spread between the youngest and the oldest. Many of his older siblings had already left home when he was born, so he couldn't even remember what they looked like let alone recall their names.

Thanks to Ancestry, Irish census information, the National Archives of Ireland and other genealogy groups, we now have the answer to most of those questions. So in addition to the stories I am going to tell you about growing up in rural Wexford in the 1940s, I am also going to share as much information as I can about our heritage on both sides of the family. So this book will be a resource for other members of the family to look into the past and hopefully add to and edit what I have already documented about the Finucanes, Rutledges, Howards and the Mullins and the many interesting stories about our immediate and extended families going back several generations.

BTF

ACKNOWLEDGEMENTS

The author would like to thank all those individuals who contributed their poems, stories, recollections and sayings in honor of Patricia Finucane on her 100th birthday. Thanks also to those who allowed me to show photographs of them in this publication. Finally, I would like to acknowledge the Swyrich Corporation for giving me permission to display images of the Finucane and Rutledge family crests on the front cover and the black and white versions of the crests at the beginning of Chapters 11 and 12.

CHAPTER 1

The Beautiful Beechville

I was born in Beechville (which was the name of the house), on the feast of St. Michael the archangel (September 29th) in 1942. I often wondered why they didn't name me Michael since I honored the archangel by arriving on his feast day. However my father's name was Michael and it was not traditional or practical to name the son after the father, for obvious reasons. So I was named Brendan. Why Brendan? Well I thought I knew the answer to that question. You see a famous distant cousin of ours, Brendan Finucane, was an ace pilot with the RAF during World War 2. Well it turned out that I wasn't named for him either. But I have maintained a steady interest in 'Spitfire Paddy's' story ever since, because he was a true Irish hero. Perhaps I will get a chance to tell you a little more about my namesake later on in the story.

I was a home delivery and one of my earliest experiences was to have surgery without anesthesia shortly after birth. Obviously I don't remember that, at least at a conscious level, but I sometimes wonder if that early experience of surgery without anesthesia may have influenced my later decision to pursue a career in anesthesia.

I have always had a very special attachment to Beechville, perhaps, because I was born there. I can actually visualize within 10 square feet where I first came into this world. The house was located about two miles north of

Wexford town, on Clonard road. My parents rented the property during the war. It was a traditional Georgian house that came with about 15 acres of good land. There were five large bedrooms upstairs and it had a very spacious landing. There was a great view of our surroundings from the bedroom windows in each room. At nighttime the light from Tuskar lighthouse, approximately 9 miles away, as the crow flies, from where we lived, would illuminate our rooms every minute or so depending upon visibility.

The lights from Tuskar

Swelled up at night

And made us wonder

'Bout the sailors' plight

(BTF 1989)

Tuskar Rock/Lighthouse is 6.8 miles off the south east coast of Wexford. According to: *Irish Wrecks Online* 176 ships have met their fate at Tuskar Rock. It is the most dangerous group of rocks in Irish coastal waters.

Aer Lingus, flight 712 from Cork, destined for London, mysteriously crashed near Tuskar on March 24th, 1968. I was the intern on call at a nearby hospital that day and I remember receiving an eerie phone call informing me about the plane crash and that casualties may be brought to our hospital. Unfortunately there were no casualties as all 61 souls perished. The cause of the crash remains a mystery to this day.

Sometimes they say a picture is worth a thousand words so let me show you a photograph of Beechville and what it looked like about 70 years ago:

Beechville

Upon entering the property from the roadway there was a gateway which we had to open upon entering or leaving. Mrs.Reddy lived in the lodge on the right hand side immediately upon passing through the gateway. She lived in that small house with her three sons, Billy, John and Ned. She was a very pleasant lady and loved her cup of 'tay' and she always minded her own business. Upon passing the entrance gateway, you then continued up the avenue towards the house then entered another gateway as you approached the front of the house. Visitors would take a left turn and ascend several steps up to the front door, which had a big knocker and the door was always green in color.

At the back of the house midway down the stairs on the left side we had an entry into the conservatory overlooking the orchard which was protected by a sturdy high wall. We had beautiful apples in the orchard. They were quite small apples but very sweet tasting and juicy. They were called Beauty of Bath apples. We also had crab apples from which we made crab apple jam. We also had gooseberry bushes and the gooseberries were very tasty and made wonderful jam.

We had really interesting neighbors. Our neighbors immediately north of us were the Fallon family. Paddy Fallon was the head of the family and his wife's name was Pinky. They had 6 boys and I was particularly friendly with Ivan and Padraig. Paddy Fallon worked with Customs and Excise in Wexford but behind the scenes he was a productive poet and playwright. We didn't know anything about that while we were growing up.

There were 6 boys in the family and they all did very well in school and college and were scholars in many disciplines. Gary was the oldest and was a veterinary surgeon like my father. Brian was an art critic and literary editor of the *Irish Times* and published 6 books. Conor was (is) an accomplished artist. Ivan is a writer and wrote a biography of Tony O'Reilly the famous Irish international rugby player. He became the Chief Executive of Independent News and Media (UK) Ltd. Padraig was the youngest member of the family. He was the Chair of *Euromoney* and the head office was based in London, UK. He created a very successful business, starting out as a financial journalist. He wrote an excellent book about growing up in Wexford entitled 'Hymn of the Dawn'. Niall Fallon was a successful writer and journalist with the *Irish Times* and a fly fishing expert. They were an amazing family.

We lived in basement of Beechville during the war. I'm not sure why, other than safety concerns as we could see evidence of bombing east of us in the night sky. The basement was very dark and dank and had a very musty smell. The room on the right hand side was the brightest and that was where we spent most of our time during the day. I remember there was a big open fireplace that came with a fan blower's wheel. The room on the far left hand side was quite dark and I remember my father sprung a well there and that's where we got our water and that's where he threatened to send us if we did not behave!

While living in the basement of our house during the war I made the occasional foray into the upper precincts of our home. I was always fascinated by a piece of furniture referred to as the 'bureau'. It had several drawers all of which were locked. Fortunately I found the key and worked my way through these drawers, one by one. During one of these explorations

I encountered a glass vial containing a yellowish-green powder which seemed fluorescent. It looked sweet to me so I tried every way I could to taste it. Eventually I took the 'bit between my teeth' and bit through the vial without cutting myself and at last the tasting began. Oh, it was the most ghastly, disgusting stuff I had ever tasted. However I did ingest a sizeable amount. My parents noticed I was missing and when they found me my face was the same color as the stuff I had just tasted. Then I learnt the bad news! I had just ingested RAT POISON. My Dad informed me that I must vomit. This was not something I could do on demand. My Dad did everything he could to make me vomit including holding me, by the legs, head first over the bannister. That didn't work either. Obviously I hadn't taken enough to kill me but it was rat poison. Hopefully there was a lesson to be learned from that experience

My sister Ann and I were very close when we were growing up in Beechville. She was just a little older than me and did her best to keep me out of trouble. When we were about 4 or 5 years of age, the powers that be decided that we were going to have our tonsils out. For some reason I thought we were going to get toys or ties. I was quite confused about the whole thing and was not ready for what transpired. I remember our Granny was visiting from Oxford and things usually happened when she visited. I don't recall being told that I was going to have an operation. It turned out to be quite an unpleasant experience. I still recall the smothering sensation I experienced while being 'put under' and also the smell of ether or chloroform. I also recall vivid dreaming about a train going through a tunnel. I subsequently learned that the anesthetic didn't 'take' and apparently I woke up in the middle of the procedure. Within the first five years of my life I had two experiences with surgery, one supposedly with an anesthetic and the other without. I must say I wasn't impressed with e(i)ther!

In retrospect I wondered why we had our tonsils out and what precipitated that decision. Rheumatic fever was quite a common illness in Ireland when we were growing up. We had our own personal experience with that disease. Our uncle Dermot died from Rheumatic heart disease when he was in his early twenties in 1944. Rheumatic fever is caused by a bacterium called streptococcus which frequently infects the tonsils. When streptococci get into the blood stream they can attack the heart or the kidney. In this day and age of antibiotics it is much simpler and safer to prescribe a medication than to perform surgery. Tonsillectomy was a very common procedure in those days and was not without risk but much less so today. Rheumatic fever and Rheumatic heart disease are rare conditions in modern times in the developed world.

Beechville was a very special place

That's where we were born

That's where we grew up

That's where we played 'hide-and-go-seek'

That's where we listened to stories huddled by the fire

That's where we were scared in the dark and saw moving shadows on the wall

That's where we laughed and cried and fought like cats and dogs

That's where we smelled the daffodils, crocuses and primroses in spring-time and listened to the cuckoo sing

That's where we picked apples and gooseberries and mushrooms

Beechville is no longer there, but its beauty lives on in our memories, never to be forgotten

(BTF 1989)

CHAPTER 2

Horse Sense

My father was a great horseman. He loved horses. He owned, trained, bred and even rode his own horses in competition. I have a great memory of him riding one of our horses at a point-to-point race in the Wexford region. I think you can get a sense of my father's great interest in horses in this next picture.

(photo, courtesy of Donna Finucane)

I loved horses too but was lacking in what my father would call 'stable manners'. My approach to horsemanship was quite simple. If I had a desire to ride a horse, it was like calling a taxi and when I was finished riding I really wasn't interested in the aftercare, which was quite demanding. The horses had to be watered and fed and groomed after an outing. Despite this failing I still loved to be with horses.

One of my earliest experiences with horses was quite unpleasant. My dad decided to mow the meadow in front of Beechville, one fine spring day when I was a youngster. In those days we used horse drawn mowers. This was my first encounter with Goffey Jones. Goffey was a large Clydesdale-like draft horse owned by Mike Doyle, a friend of my Dad's. I was about 6 or 7 years old at the time. Goffey Jones was a grand, reliable, obedient and tame but huge white horse. We started early in the morning on a beautiful spring day in May. I mounted Goffey at about 8 a.m. and rode him bare-back until sundown. I clearly remember the cuckoo singing all day as they do in May and there is nothing quite like the smell of freshly mown hay.

Remember the smell

Of freshly mown hay,

We could always tell

'T was the month of May

Remember the cuckoos'

Cacophonous calls

And the sound of the moos

O'er the barnyard walls

(BTF 1989)

When I dismounted at dusk I felt quite stiff and then I went to the bath-room and discovered that I was unable to void but there was no urgency to do so at this stage. I informed my parents about this new symptom and they were quite amused at first, but they became far more concerned when I still could not void at bedtime. They were in full panic mode the following morning at breakfast when I informed them that nothing was forthcoming. The desire to void was there but 'mother nature' was not co-operating. My parents were distraught at this time and were ready to call Pax Sinnott our GP. He was the last person I wanted to see, so emer-gency measures began. My parents made me stand in readiness over the toilet with all the taps in the sink and bath in the full 'on' position. My parents and two sisters were all there chanting PEE, PEE, PEE! After a while they all left as the results were very disappointing. But I was told that I must stay there until I voided no matter how long it was going to take. I was feeling pretty uncomfortable at this stage, bursting would be a good way of describing how I felt. After what felt like a very long time, the eerie silence in the bathroom was broken by a loud, rumbling sound like a charging elephant. Terrified as I was I looked back and saw my fa-ther charging towards me shouting at the top of his voice-'if you don't pee now boy, I'm going to give you a belt of this thorny stick'. He frightened the daylights out of me and in the midst of all the kerfuffle I noticed that I was peeing but was missing the target by a wide margin. However that transgression was forgiven on this occasion. I peed for what felt like half-an-hour. I'll never forget how relieved I was on that occasion and so was everyone else.

Horsemanship was important in our family and after my experience rid-ing a horse all day I learnt the importance of riding with a saddle. As a result of that incident I have always been a slow starter of the micturition process. Fast forward about 40 years. I remember having a minor surgical procedure under spinal anesthesia. Afterwards I was very slow to void and the surgical resident informed me that if I didn't void soon he was going to have to catheterize me! I was not happy with that idea. So I told him that I had a treatment for that problem. He was very interested until I told him it would require a trip to the liquor store for a six pack of beer. He very reluctantly followed my instructions and after one beer as they say I was 'peeing like a racehorse'!

The Finucanes were never snobs but they were very particular when it came to horsemanship. We dressed impeccably on those occasions and at an early age we learnt how to sit properly on a horse (straight, upright back) and how to hold the reins between your fingers. My dad was a real enthusiast. He used to throw me up on thoroughbred yearlings like a sack of potatoes. I invariably ended up on my rear end on the ground. I had no fear of horses after that. I finally progressed to fox hunting which was one of the most exhilarating sports I have ever tried. I'll never forget the power of a horse in full gallop. My career as a horseman came to a grinding halt when I was sent to boarding school at age 10. My favorite horse was a chestnut gelding named Red Feathers. My first real riding experience, other than Goffy Jones, was riding a little white pony named Wilkie.

This reminds me of another story that I must share with you involving Wilkie. We had relatives visiting from Dublin and they wanted to ride Wilkie and we were happy to let them do so. First up was our cousin from Dublin and she was about 12 years old. We put her up on the pony and things were going well for a while and then all of a sudden Wilkie decided he wanted to go back to his stable and took off like a rocket, galloping at high speed through narrow spaces and we chased after him. We arrived just in time to witness the disaster that was about to happen. Wilkie was a small pony and he ran into the stable but to our horror the upper stable door was still closed. Fortunately the rider, our cousin, put up her two hands to avoid being slammed into the door. Needless to say she came off the pony with a thud. Fortunately she was not hurt. The image of that happening still remains vividly in my mind and reminds me of the saying about 'closing the stable door after the horse has bolted'. Our version of that well known cliché states that: 'it is important to keep the stable door open in case the horse decides to return prematurely'!

One of the things that we as a family really enjoyed was going to the races, especially when one of our own horses was running. One of our family's greatest equine triumphs was the day that Selskar Baby won at the Wexford races. This would have been sometime in the 1950s. My dad was not a betting man himself but my mum had the occasional 'flutter' when we attended a race meeting. My dad approached me that evening at the races and asked if I had any money and I said 'I have ten shillings'. He said 'put it all on the horse'. The odds were very good. The bookies were offering 20/1. So I put it all on the horse and she came in first! We were all shocked out of our minds except my father who knew she was going to win. I'll never forget the scene in our house that evening when my Mum opened her handbag. She snapped open her bag and it was loaded with pound notes (punts) and they were flying out in every direction, all over the room. I was very happy with my own tenner too. What a great moment for our family. My dad knew the horse was going to win but he only told his family. He got the cold shoulder from many of his 'friends' for a long time after that incident.

My dad developed a reputation for his clinical abilities especially when it came to diagnosing lameness in horses. Horsemen came from near and far seeking his opinion. He had a great way with horses. He was a 'Horse Whisperer'. Whenever he was consulted about a horse he would stand back and take a look at the whole animal. Then he would approach the horse and rub the neck and talk gently to them. Then he would examine them from head to toe making the odd inspiratory sound as he extracted information from his clients. He was a master at this game.

We always had a couple of brood mares at home. 'Bock' was one of our favorites. She never raced because she had a very crooked foreleg. But she was a great brood mare. I think she was Selskar Baby's dam. My dad would handle the foaling procedure himself with a little help from us.

My dad always had a great ambition to breed a Derby winner (Epsom or Irish) or failing that a Grand National winner. Well he didn't quite do either. He became so well known in the equine business he decided that he needed a gimmick. So he bought himself an ophthalmoscope. After several months I asked him how his clients liked the ophthalmoscope. He said they loved it. He gave me a demonstration one day and it was then that I noticed that he was shining the light in his own eye. His response to that was 'it's no wonder I couldn't see a thing but it sure does impress the farmers'!

My father bred one very good thoroughbred horse named Selskar Abbot. I think he was born in 1948. He was a very frisky, black yearling. I remember him running around our lawn with a teddy bear in his mouth. My dad sold Selskar Abbot at the yearling sales in Ballsbridge, Dublin for around 500 guineas. The buyer eventually sold Selskar Abbot to King George VI.

According to the Bank of England one Pound sterling in 1950 was the equivalent to 20 pounds sterling, today. Using the same calculation 500 guineas was worth approximately 11,000 pounds sterling in today's money. Selskar Abbot was subsequently sold to King George VI and won about 50,000 guineas for the Crown during his racing career. That would be the equivalent of one million pounds sterling today!!

I recently 'googled' the name Selskar Abbot to see if there was any information about him on the internet and indeed there was. There was a book written about Churchill's famous horse, Colonist II, by Fred Glueckstein. In that book I noted that Colonist II was scheduled to run in the Winston Churchill Stakes in Hurst Park on May 14th 1951. Also competing in that race, were two of King George VI's horses, Above Board and Selskar Abbot. Churchill's horse won that day beating Above Board by two lengths. Selskar Abbot did not place. That evening the King sent Churchill a telegram from Balmoral Castle saying 'Many congratulations on your win' and Churchill responded saying: 'I'm deeply grateful for your Majesty's most kind and gracious telegram'. I'm sure my dad would have enjoyed hearing that story at the time! We all certainly did about 70 years later!

My dad was never a great supporter of royalty but he greatly respected people who were interested in horses and I know that he was very proud of his great achievement breeding Selskar Abbot. He was a happy man during the Abbot's reign. Selskar Abbot had a strange ending. He was found dead in his stable one morning in late January 1952. About a week later the King himself passed away. My dad's comment was priceless-'Ah sure we know why the King died, he was broken hearted after the Abbot passed'!! King George VI died on February 6th 1952.

Following is a photograph of Selskar Abbot racing, I'm not sure where, but the photograph was taken by a photographer from the *Irish Times,* who gave me permission to publish this picture. It was a very close race but I don't think Selskar Abbot won. I suspect this event took place around 1950 before Selskar Abbot was sold to the King.

I have one final horse related story to tell you and I think you'll enjoy it. We were living in Edmonton, Alberta at the time in the early 1990s. My son Mickey was visiting us at the time. There was a Gun Show on at Northlands and he was quite interested in guns at the time. Upon leaving the Gun Show I heard a familiar refrain in the background: 'And they're off' so I quickly concluded that there was horse racing at Northlands race track. I thought the kids would be interested. Conor was with us also and was about 7 at the time. Obviously we missed at least one race but I assured Mickey and Conor that there would be other races. We waited at the finish line for the horses to come in in the next races. I explained to the kids that we couldn't see where the horses started because it was too far away. We heard when the horses were under orders and we heard 'and they're off'. I told Mickey and Conor that we should see the horses anytime now and after a few minutes Mickey said 'Dad, where are the horses?' and this old guy besides us leaned over the railing and said: 'the horses are in Calgary' with a big grin on his face. Silly me! This was a simulcast from Calgary. I was mercilessly teased about that incident for years afterwards. My dad really enjoyed that story and when he visited us in Edmonton a few years later, I took him to the Canadian Derby and at the entrance to Northlands race track he asked the officials: 'will there be horses here today?'

CHAPTER 3

The Hounds of Our Homes

One of my earliest memories as a child was playing with our dogs. We always had one or more dogs around the house. Lanky was one of the first dogs I remember and then we had Judy. Then we had Bambi, a Welsh corgi. Bambi was a very tough little dog and totally fearless. I remember a pack of mongrels found their way on to our property one summer's day. There were about six of them including a very scrawny greyhound. Bambi was surrounded by these dogs and was not in least bit intimidated by their numbers. My dad happened to be clipping the hedge in front of Beechville at the time. Without much warning he 'let fly' with the hedge clippers in the direction of the attacking pack of dogs. The hedge clippers struck the greyhound right in the chest and it sounded very hollow, much like a drum. The greyhound dropped to the ground like a stone and after a few seconds got up and ran off like a scalded cat. The other dogs followed suit and ran off terrified with Bambi nipping at their heels.

One of my favorite dogs was named Jeremy. One of my dad's clients gave him an Irish Wolf Hound. He was really quite small as a pup but grew very fast. By the time he was 6 months old he was like a small pony. He was amazingly gentle with children and had a voracious appetite. In those days animals were fed left-overs. We didn't have commercially produced dog food in those days. Jeremy became my dog and he followed me everywhere. I used to ride my bike to mass in Rowe Street Church most days and despite my orders not to follow me, he would wait for several minutes and then would take off after me. He was so big and strong he could open the very large church doors using his front paws. He would then come bounding into the church looking for me and when he found me he would rise up and rest his front paws on the side of the pew and start howling with joy. I then had the unenviable task of escorting him out of the church as he barked and made a big fuss of me. I remember I was so embarrassed when this happened and it usually occurred when the priest was giving a sermon. I would skulk out of the church with a big red face on me and if looks could kill I'd be dead long ago. I was about 9 or 10 years old at the time.

It soon became quite apparent that Jeremy's dietary needs far exceeded what we fed him in scraps. It soon became clear that Jeremy had another source of food. He would return from one of his hunting outings with feathers adhering to his mouth region. I then realized he wasn't just chasing chickens he was eating them. I was concerned but didn't really appreciate the implications at the time. Then the rumors that he was interested in sheep were spreading. It really wasn't great publicity to hear that the local vet's dog was killing sheep, although my dad and I did not believe that rumor. Then a terrible thing happened. Jeremy went missing one day out of the blue. It was a terrible shock to me that this would happen. My dad and I looked high and low for him without success. I was heart-broken. Not long after this tragedy I was sent off to boarding school. It took me a long time to forget Jeremy. This was the first great loss I had experienced in life and it was compounded by the fact that we never found him!

There is an epilogue to this story. Many years later, but while we still lived in Beechville, I said to my mother 'I'd give anything to find out what happened to Jeremy' and my mother said 'you are standing right over where Jeremy was buried many, many years ago'. So I finally found out what happened. My mother said he had to be put down. Jeremy had developed a taste for killing chickens and other small prey. She then admitted that she did the deed. She said 'it was quite painless. I'd seen your father do it many times'. An injection of chloroform into the lung was a very pleasant way to go. It was quick and painless and lethal in about 15 minutes.

After I left home my mother got another dog and named him Kissy. Kissy was a Cavalier King Charles Spaniel. They are very popular dogs and among the few that are allowed into restaurants in the UK. In 1984 I was visiting from America with the family and we were invited to a Country Fair in Clonegal near Bunclody, County Wexford. It was a great event. They also had a Dog Show and my mother entered Kissy for the competition. I remember my sister was visiting from Wales and she was asked to be the judge of the Dog Show. Well guess who won first prize? Kissy of course! I think this ensuing photo tells the story better than anything I write!

Dog Show, Clonegal, 1984

I have some other dog stories to tell you. When we lived in Atlanta, in the 1970s I was given a dog by a friend whose husband had died suddenly. Boris was the dog's name. He was a beautiful Samoyed. He had a fabulous, thick white coat. He was well behaved and very gentle with children. But he did not like to be contained. Shortly after we got him he escaped and we got a call the next day informing us that they had found our dog. He had wandered about 6 miles away apparently pursuing a dog in heat. We did everything to stop him from wandering. We had a fenced backyard and we reinforced the fence with chicken wire to no avail. Our neighbor down the road complained that our dog was loose so we electrified the fence. The neighbor then complained that we had electrified the fence! It still didn't stop Boris from escaping. He was a pure breed and high on the American Kennel Club (AKC) list, so we bred him and he sired a litter of

5 or 6 pups and we got the pick of the litter and we named him Ivan. He was Donna's dog. Unfortunately he was hit by a car in our neighborhood and killed. Donna was heartbroken for months afterwards. Eventually I got another Samoyed for Donna for her next birthday. His name was Victor and he was a great companion for Boris. They were both escape artists and developed an interest in chasing cats. Eventually they were not just chasing cats. Donna would call me at work and whisper into the phone 'there is a dead cat on our front lawn, what shall I do?' We were expecting a complaint from one of our neighbors but we never heard anything. Does this story sound familiar? Obviously something had to be done.

We really did out best to keep our dogs off the street but there was the occasional breach. I remember one morning we got a call at about 6 a.m. from one of our neighbors complaining that the dogs were loose and she advised us to bring the dogs to a doggie psychiatrist!! She was serious!

Another neighbor complained to us that Boris had broken her dog's hip! Her dog was a very large poodle mongrel weighing about 50 pounds more than Boris. We argued vehemently that it was highly unlikely that Boris did this. It just didn't make sense. The bill for the hip replacement was about $600. Eventually we agreed to pay half the fee just for peace sake within the neighborhood. We were not very happy about this settlement. Subsequently our neighbor's dog bit the owner quite badly on the leg. We blamed the 'Irish curse' for that happening.

We had an opportunity to go on sabbatical to Ireland in 1984 so we had to decide what to do with the dogs. My secretary had a farm in North Georgia and she offered to mind the dogs when we were away. When we returned my secretary had already found a new job and she was quite happy to keep the dogs on her farm and our children did not seem to miss the dogs so we said 'c'est la vie'. However that sentiment did not last very long and our daughter Erin begged us to get another dog. Erin was about 6 year's old at the time. So we asked her to research what kind of dog we should get. Erin arrived at the conclusion that we should get a Golden Retriever. So we answered an advertisement for a Golden Retriever and that's how we got our last dog and we named her Nikki and from the beginning we insisted that she would be an outdoor dog. We got her when she was about 6 months old. She was a pure breed and had excellent credentials from AKC. Shortly after we got her she fell about 30 feet from out deck in Atlanta but landed on her feet none the worse for wear.

We moved to Alberta in 1989 and we wondered about how well she would tolerate very cold temperatures. We had a very good dog house made for her by Tom McIntosh while we were in Georgia and brought it with us to Alberta. In the winter we filled the dog house with straw and added further heat by hooking up an electric light in the doghouse. During the winter Nikki's fur increased in thickness and she never had any trouble with the cold temperatures even when they went as low as -40 C. Nikki was a fabulous dog in every way and a good watch dog and very gentle with children. She was a great companion. We used to ride out bikes down into Terwilleger Park in Edmonton and she would follow us closely. Whenever I stopped she would stop and the kids would ride off and call her but she would not leave unless I did. I'm grateful to Alex Cubitt for walking Nikki and taking her on hunting trips when I was very busy. Nikki was a very healthy dog and the only time she got sick it was serious. She suddenly started losing weight and was failing to thrive and did not want to eat. So I brought her to the vet and they checked her out and kept her overnight. The following morning I went to pick her up and they said they couldn't release her because she had an intravenous line and I said I could take care of that myself. At this stage I had paid about $800 for 24 hours of care, I asked the vet what was wrong and he said she probably has cancer and they were going to do an exploratory operation. I told them that I would take her home and that I didn't want to put her through a big procedure at age 15. Nikki was well for another two weeks and we noticed that she was failing to thrive again and began to vomit and lose weight. So we decided to take her out of her misery and have her put down. Kevin and I brought her to the local vet and they gave her, her final shot. It was very sad but we did what was best for our dog. That evening the family left on a vacation to Mexico which softened the blow for everyone.

We have great memories of the dogs in our lives and we have been very lucky with the animals that were a big part of our lives for many years.

In retirement we have not yet found a need for another dog to share our lives with, but that could change with time. We play a lot of golf. It's not fair to keep a dog cooped up all day, so no more dogs for us until we can't play golf anymore!

CHAPTER 4

What Did You Say?

I remember the time when Beechville was wired for electricity. I also remember when we first had the telephone installed. The phone number was 260 and it was a shared or party line. These events took place in the mid-1940s.

Before the advent of the telephone the farmers would come to our house walking, biking, in a horse and trap or rarely in a motor vehicle to seek my father's advice about a problem with one of their animals. My dad was a large animal veterinary surgeon and didn't have much time for small animal practice mainly because of the people associated with it. However he would never turn a client away and was always very civil to the public. The 'townies' as we called then frequently came to him for help when their dogs were choking on a bone. There wasn't anything he couldn't do with a little freezing, a penknife and some ammonia. I remember one incident when he removed an impacted bone from the esophagus of a small dog. The dog had a cardiac arrest during the procedure so my dad shouted at me to get the ammonia. A couple of whiffs later the dog was up and about-clearly a case of intense vagal stimulation! The client returned for a post-operative visit a few days later and seemed grateful and asked if there was anything we could do to stop the milk form leaking out through the dog's neck. A few stitches later the animal was up and about with no further leakage from the wound. The client said 'and how much do I owe you sir' and my dad said 'ah three and sixpence will cover it!'

My dad was a very popular vet. He loved talking to the farmers and vice versa. Not very much money exchanged hands because money was very scarce in those days. Quite often he would be paid in kind. My mum kept the books and she had stacks of books of unpaid bills going back to pre-war days in the 1930s. We had the Irish version of 'All Creatures Great and Small' right in our own back yard. The late night call was the bane of my dad's life. On many a night I was awakened from a deep slumber, only to hear my father and the farmer engage in a loud animated conversation. Mick would lower the bedroom window and greet the farmer with a loud bellow, 'what the hell do you want at this hour of the night?' I'll never forget one particular conversation I overheard. Mick asked 'what's wrong' and the farmer answered 'the sow has lost her suck'. And Mick answered with a torrent of abuse. But quite often he would get up and go out on the call. We all knew to keep our mouths shut the following morning. Breakfast on those mornings was a silent, sober affair.

When I reached the age of reason I began to earn my keep. I washed dishes, milked the cows and answered the telephone. Communication via the telephone on a party line was quite challenging in the early days. A farmer would call in with a message for the vet and I would answer the phone. There was nothing wrong with my hearing but when I answered the phone I couldn't for the life of me understand what some of these farmers were saying most of the time. As my mother would say 'a lot of these people swallow their words' and all the words ran together. I would ask them to repeat the message several times despite this I invariably ended up with a badly garbled message for my dad. Of course when he returned, he would say 'were there any calls?' I dreaded these moments because it usually ended up in a one sided, shouting match.

Following is a facsimile of an exchange between a farmer and me:

Farmer: HEOIIDDVIHIN (Translation) hello, is the vet in?

Brendan: WHO IS SPEAKING PLEASE?

Farmer: OBRIENOBALLINABUGA! #*@&<>?$%

Brendan: COULD YOU REPEAT THAT PLEASE

Farmer: YEAHEWAHEREINTHEFAL Yea, he was here in the fall!

Brendan: I'M SORRY I CANT HEAR YOU

Farmer: IDDISDIMISSIS! (Translation): Is this the Missus?

Brendan: NO THIS IS HIS SON

Farmer: YADEWEDDERISGRATE! (Translation): Yea, the weather is great!

This will give you an idea of what I was up against. That conversation with the farmer could translate into anything by the time it passed from the farmer and several miles of telephone cable, with the ocean, braying animals and noisy children in the background. Please bear in mind that the farmers were not totally familiar with this new method of communication and sometimes spoke into the receiving end of the telephone. By the time I was finished talking to the farmer I was lucky if I got his surname right. Quite often there would be four or five Mick O'Brien's listed in the phone book.

These confrontations with my Dad, over faulty telephone messages, became so troublesome that I would hide rather than answer the phone. As a result of these tormenting experiences, answering the phone as a child, I now have a condition called *'telephonophobia'*, defined as a severe dread of answering the phone. Consequently I now only make calls and will go to great lengths not to answer the phone! With 'call display' available on most phones these days, I never answer the phone unless I know who is calling. It is quite amazing how telecommunications have progressed during the past 70 years or so.

CHAPTER 5

Shank's Mare

The Finucanes were always great walkers and I was no exception, but I still had trouble keeping up with my dad. He had a very brisk pace indeed.

I very quickly learned how to ride a bicycle. I rode to school every morning, which was about 2 miles when I started in the 'Boker' (school) in Wexford town, which was located very near Bride Street church. I went home for lunch every day. By the time I was finished school and back home in the afternoon I would have cycled about 8 miles each day. In retrospect what better preparation can one get to be an athlete.

One thing really bothered me about cycling and that was the appearance of my bike. It just looked plain ugly, especially the saddle. My friend up the road with whom I used to play hurling, had a brand new bike and they were not wealthy people and I quite resented that, especially when he kept asking me when I was going to get a new bike. So I started a campaign to replace my bike. I tried a number of ploys. I did my best to lose my bike on several occasions by leaving it at various locations. That bike was so ugly even the tinkers wouldn't steal it. It got to the point that I could not remember where I left my bike half of the time until I needed it for school. Quite often I would leave it by the wall on the public road and I would hop over the wall and take a short cut to the house. At last my bike was reported missing and I couldn't wait to share this information with my parents. I gleefully reported this incident to my parents who were not at all amused. I assumed that I would be driven to school the following morning. I was wrong about that. I had to get up 30 minutes earlier because I had to walk to school. Furthermore I had to take a packed lunch with me because I would not have sufficient time to go home for lunch. This change in routine was quite burdensome. At the same time I couldn't wait to get my new bike. So my strategy worked or so I thought. Well I was wrong. I was tersely informed that I was not getting a new bike, that I deliberately abandoned my bike and acted irresponsibly and if I could not take care of my old bike there was no sense getting me a new one. Six whole weeks went by and I was still on Shank's Mare. My plan backfired badly. The 4 mile walk to and from school, in hail rain or snow became a painful exercise and was pure drudgery.

Six weeks went by and there was no sign of a change in my parents' icy approach to this issue. 'My dad's response to my appeals was: 'You made your bed boy, now lie on it.' One evening I innocently said to my dad,' I'd give anything to have my old crock back'. Then he said your bike must be around here somewhere. So we went out to the hay-barn and started looking around. Suddenly he said 'I think I found your bike' and he proceeded to fork some hay out of the way and low and behold there was my bike. He said 'lucky the horses needed some hay or we might never have found it' Gosh I was so happy to have my bike back and very grateful to my dad for finding it. I never did get a new bike but after what I went through I was delighted to have my old 'crock' back and I also think that I learnt a good lesson. You don't really appreciate what you are missing until you don't have it anymore!

I must say I still liked Martin Buggy's bike better but I got over it. Martin and I used to swap bikes and race on our way back to school. One day I overdid it on Martin's bike. I was speeding down the big hill just beyond the football park approaching White Rock when a man stepped out from behind a lorry parked on the road, wheeling his bicycle up the hill at a snail's pace. I crashed into him with Martin's bike. I could see his front wheel buckle like a bucket handle right in front of my eyes as I cart wheeled over the handlebars. I have never seen anyone so angry. He looked like a total madman frothing at the mouth and he threatened me with the police. He terrorized me so I gave him my name and address and got on the bike and went back to school. I didn't tell my parents what happened. The next day I recognized that same angry man walking up our driveway so I blurted out the story to my mother who didn't look in the least bit concerned. I heard a loud angry knock on the door and my mother opened it. There he was standing with the buckled wheel in his hand showing her what I had done. My mother proceeded to give this grown man the biggest dressing down he probably ever got in his life. She told him he should be ashamed of himself picking on a little schoolboy. She ran him off the property and told him never to come back. I think he was scared of my mother. I decided to change my return route to school after that and so I went down Summer Hill past the Bishop's residence. I didn't want to meet that man again because he looked a bit crazy!

CHAPTER 6

An Gluaisteán

Just in case you don't understand the meaning of the title of this chapter, 'An Gluaisteán' is a Gaelic term for 'The Car.'

Transportation was always a bit of a problem in our house especially during the war years. I remember my father having to visit his clients on his bicycle sometimes during the war. Of course gasoline was rationed at that time. He always seemed to have problems with his jalopy. He seemed to have a lot of trouble getting his cars to start and he used the starting handle on a regular basis.

I went through a time when I worried about my dad when he was late coming home from work. I used to fret about something happening to him. I remember one occasion very well when he was late. It was close to midnight when he got home. He looked like he had just seen a ghost, and the car was a little muddier than usual. He drove a Vauxhall at the time. After a while he told me what happened. He was driving along the road at a normal speed and suddenly he had no control over the steering wheel. He went right off the road and rolled over into a field. So he turned off the engine and got out of the car which was quite difficult because the car was upside down. He got his medical bag and walked across the fields to his client who was just a couple of miles away. When he came back there was a big crowd around the car and they were looking for the body. He was none the worse for wear. With the help of some able bodied farmers they turned the car right side up and Mick got in, started her up and drove her back on to the road and home. In retrospect I wondered if he had encountered a patch of black ice.

He had some interesting ideas about wear and tear. He was totally opposed to fast driving so he always drove at around 30 MPH. He recommended keeping the tires quite flat and he wasn't a big fan of oil and filter changes.

I remember when I was about 15 my dad decided to teach me to drive. What a terrifying experience that was. He was supremely confident of my abilities as a driver and to be honest with you I was terrified. I felt like I had a lethal weapon in my hands. Of course our yard was not ideally suited for a learner driver. I'll try to describe the scene for you. The garage was on the right hand side of the house. After entering the gateway to the garage, there was a bit of an incline, which dead ended, into a whitewashed wall. In order to enter the garage you had to make a sharp, 90 degree left hand turn. The next hazard required you to stop the car quite abruptly after you entered the garage otherwise you drove down three steep steps towards the basement. I didn't get to test the second hazard because I ran smack into the whitewashed wall at about 20 MPH. So that was the end of my first lesson. Eventually I got the hang of driving but I missed out on some important lessons. I wasn't very impressed with the need for a hand brake.

The following story illustrates the importance of the hand brake and I now fully appreciate its importance. My dad sent me on an errand to pick up some Sweet Afton cigarettes. So he handed me the keys of his relatively new Austin A35. I drove to Ned Hopkin's shop on the top of Hill Street and parked the car. When I came out of the shop the car was nowhere to be seen. I couldn't figure out what happened. I thought someone might have stolen the car! Suddenly I was approached by a middle aged woman who said 'Hey mister is that your car?' and she pointed down the hill. I was shocked to see the car up on the footpath half way down the hill, prevented from going further down the hill, by a telephone pole. There was quite a big dent in the right wing of the car. This was a serious error on my part. I had parked the car in neutral gear, facing downhill and had not applied the handbrake. This was a costly error but thankfully no one was injured. My dad was not very happy about this and I was banned from driving for quite some time after that incident.

I learned some additional lessons from my next driving incident. I was an intern at Ardkeen Hospital in 1967. I didn't have a car when I graduated but my friend Kevin Walshe lent me his Morris Minor as he was going to be out of the country for some time. One night I was driving from Tramore on to the Dunmore road, when I had an accident about which I remember absolutely nothing. We didn't have seat belts in those days. Apparently I was found on the side of the road by the local GP, Dr. Keogh who brought me to Ardkeen Hospital where I worked at the time. My colleague and friend, Fineen Houlihan was on call in the emergency room that night and it was he who stitched me up. According to him, I did not need any freezing! I, to this day have no recollection of the accident. Dr. Keogh found me lying on the road several meters from the car. I clearly was concussed. The next morning I did rounds and met the people who were involved in the crash. It was quite an unpleasant experience as the lady had an ugly gash on her forehead. Fortunately no one was seriously injured. My borrowed car was a 'write off'. In fact I had to pay to have the car removed to the wreckers. I finally got around to calling home and found out that my mother already knew what happened as there was a small column in the *Irish Times* that morning with the following heading: DOCTOR FROM ARDKEEN HOSPITAL INVOLVED IN A MOTOR VEHICLE ACCIDENT and below the heading was a brief description of what had happened, including my name. Obviously someone from the hospital had called the newspaper informing them of the incident. My friend Kevin Walshe was not very happy about this either, as his car was 'totaled'. I had a significant concussion and was very lucky that no one was seriously hurt. The final outcome: I was fined £3 for careless driving and I had to pay my friend the replacement value of the car. Many years later I drove on that same stretch of road and it is still a very dangerous junction to this very day.

Everyone agrees that my father was a very smart man but on occasion even he slipped up! He and my Mum were going on a trip to Kerry to visit relatives most likely for a funeral. My Mum suggested that there was a leak in the petrol tank, evidenced by a significant accumulation of liquid on the ground when the car was stationary. My dad, being the skeptic that he was, had to see for himself. The light wasn't very good under the car so he did the unforgivable thing and lit a match—Boom! No one was hurt but my mum saw her car go up in flames right in front of her eyes! In all fairness to my dad, I never heard his side of the story. I'll have to wait a few more years to hear about that!

One of the scariest moments I have ever had driving a car was in Edmonton, Alberta in 2003. I was driving on the Whitemud Drive going west on a very cold day in February. Without warning my car slid across three lanes of very heavy traffic and came to a halt just short of the barrier separating the east bound traffic. It was like as if the steering had completely failed (does this story sound familiar?) I was driving a Mercedes at the time and the car barely touched the rear end of another car. After inspection we both agreed that there was no reportable damage to either car. Black ice is always a danger when driving in the winter in Edmonton.

I have one final story about driving cars except this time I was not the driver. Donna (wife) and I were somewhere in Arizona at a meeting. We were awakened at about three o'clock in the morning by a phone call and were informed that out daughter Erin was involved in a road traffic accident in Edmonton. The only information we received was that 'your daughter is in hospital, unconscious and in a neck brace'. There was nothing we could do except wait to fly out first thing the following morning. Fortunately when we got back to Edmonton the news was good. Erin was safe and conscious with no broken bones and no neck injury. She and her friends (eight of them altogether) were driving my Cutlass Supreme on an icy road and got into a skid and lost control of the vehicle which turned over and finally came to a halt. Mercifully no one was seriously hurt (Thank God). The vehicle was unrecognizable! I got this information second hand from my wife as I did not want to see the condition of my vehicle and visualize what could have happened.

CHAPTER 7

Do Something Religious

The Irish people were typically very religious people when we were growing up, in 1940s and 1950s. Many people went to Mass and received communion on a daily basis. We typically said Grace before meals and went down on our knees to pray before we went to bed each night. I remember there was a very popular priest in Ireland at that time who led a campaign to promote more prayer and his motto was 'the family that prays together, stays together'. Ireland like other countries around the world had its fair share of marital discord, blamed on Hollywood and other influences. The problem that we had in Ireland at the time was that divorce was not legal and did not become legal in Ireland until 1996.

As a result of Father Peyton's influence many families in Ireland said the rosary on their knees each night after supper. We did this reluctantly and had many discussions with our parents to abandon this practice but we were not successful. So each night after supper we each found a comfortable chair to bury our heads in while we prayed on our knees. We would say the rosary each night which consisted of several prayers repeated many times and took about 45 minutes to complete. It really was a very boring exercise. Occasionally one of us would have a fit of the giggles but that was usually suppressed by our Dad who would get very annoyed. This practice of praying went on for the best part of a year until we had an incident during prayers that brought a firm halt to the family rosary.

Let me explain what happened. As I mentioned before most of our daily activity inside the house took place in one room-the kitchen. It was the warmest room in the house. We had an anthracite burning stove (ESSE) in the kitchen which heated the whole house. On the evening in question Thisbee, our Siamese cat was resting on a shelf above the stove as she was accustomed to doing. On this particular evening we were boiling water in a pot on the stove. Thisbee awoke suddenly and appeared to lose her footing and to avoid falling into the pot of boiling water she took an escape route and sprang onto my father's back while he was praying. There was an immediate outburst of spontaneous laughter from the whole family and we all thought that this was a sign from the spirits that it was time to discontinue this practice in our family and there were no objections!

I was quite taken by the church as a young man and was a daily mass goer and communicant for many years while I was in boarding school. The school was run by Presentation Brothers and they spent a lot of time trying to recruit young boys into the brotherhood. These recruitment efforts started when we were about 11 or 12 years old. I, like many of my confreres, was subjected to these lengthy indoctrinations and when I was about 15 I told my mother that I was going to become a Presentation Brother. I could tell she was quite upset especially when I asked her to help me complete the paperwork. I finally gave up on that idea when my mother ignored my various requests to complete the necessary paperwork. One of my very best friends at Presentation College, Bray, Noel Clarke, actually made up his mind to become a priest and to go on the Maynooth Missions to China. So I dropped the idea of being a brother and was now considering becoming a priest.

In my final year at school, I was really quite confused about a career and although I had seriously considered becoming a priest, I decided on becoming an engineer because I really enjoyed math. Two of my classmates, Trevor Mc Gill and Ned Wilson, decided they wanted to go to medical school and we all got together one day before we graduated and they convinced me that Medicine would be a better option for me. My mother was quite relieved on the one hand that I wasn't entering the church but neither of my parents was totally sold on the idea of me doing Medicine.

My father finally said that if I wanted to do Medicine I had to pass the Trinity Matriculation exam. I had sufficient points from my Leaving Certificate to enter Medical School and in fact for 5 pounds (punts) I could buy the Trinity Matric, which was an equivalent qualification to what I already had. My father was quite adamant that if I wanted to go to medical school I had to sit the exam, so I did and I passed! But that is not the end of the story.

Pre-Med was a big stumbling block before one went on to study Medicine at UCD. All of those students interested in Medicine and Dentistry had a to pass the Pre-Med exam, which consisted of an intense course of study involving 4 subjects, Botany, Zoology, Physics and Chemistry. There were about 300 students competing for 150 positions in Medicine or Dentistry. So it was quite competitive. Having spent 8 years in boarding school I was not used to the freedoms of attending university. I found very nice 'digs' with the Waters family on Donore Avenue, just off the South Circular Road within easy reach of Earlsfort Terrace and very close to my three great aunts who lived at 32 Raymond Terrace, South Circular Road.

I really enjoyed this new found freedom and I did study hard initially but not hard enough. By February or March of the following year, with exams looming I realized that I needed a backup plan if I failed Pre-Med. So I began to reconsider the priesthood idea again. The trouble was that if you failed Pre-Med you could not continue in UCD. Once you were out, you were out for good bringing great shame to the family!

My dad was quite amused by my change of heart and said it was a good plan and that I would always have somewhere to stay as a priest. I would get a free car and membership in the golf club and I would have free maid service and I would never have to worry about money again. However he did give me one piece of advice. He said, in case I changed my mind it was a good idea to study hard and try to pass the exam. I did take that advice and it was good advice because once I got the results of the exam the idea of becoming a priest was no longer a discussion.

CHAPTER 8

A Prince of a Man

Our father was a quiet, almost reclusive, individual who never enjoyed big crowds or any type of fussing and couldn't stand eating out anywhere and in the latter years absolutely detested driving. He would always say 'Why would I bother going out to a restaurant or hotel when I have the best cook in Ireland right here in my own back yard.' This used to drive my mother crazy because she had to wait for us to grow up before anyone took her out to dinner. The truth was that our mum was a gourmet cook.

Our dad was a creature of habit. He got up at the same time every day, drank his glass of warm water and went to bed at the same time every night. He ate the same food each day and rarely ever drank alcohol. My mum was almost driven insane with the monotony of it and loved when one of us came home so she could experiment a little.

He was a great storyteller and had a wonderful sense of humor. He read the newspaper from cover to cover every day. He was a great defender of the underdog and loved to play the devil's advocate in many discussions. He had a lot of interesting ideas. He was dead against insurance. He had little time for the banks and distrusted politicians and the Church. He rebelled against the Church when they published the tithes in the local newspaper. He was no great fan of the British either until he had grandchildren who were British. He hadn't much time for Royalty either but respected the Queen because she was a horsey person. He was a great fan of Mohamed Ali. He was very distrustful of information from most sources. He claimed that Armstrong walking on the moon was a hoax! We all had great fun with that one!

He maintained that the world was full of 'chancers' and lawyers were among the worst (when he said lawyer, it sounded like 'liar'. He said 'never go to law because even when you win you lose.' He maintained that some of these so called experts in various professions 'don't know enough to know how little they knew.' He also was of the opinion that 5% of the people in the world controlled 95% of the people. Another one of his favorite sayings was: 'Everyone is your potential enemy until proven otherwise and there are no exceptions.'

He was known as Mick by most people except his children, so to keep things simple I will call him Mick from now on in my writing of this chapter. He had some great sayings and I'll share them with you as follows: 'Tell no man your business, especially the priest and the peeler'. He was not a great fan of the banks either and he would say 'A bank manager's handshake is as sincere as a prostitute's kiss'. British justice was another one of his pet peeves especially when it came to Irish politics. He would say 'the Brits would give you an anesthetic before they slit your throat'. He had another great saying too when some of these so called experts (armchair politicians) pontificated on some topic they knew little about, he would say, 'He's like a lighthouse on a bog, brilliant but useless.'

Mick used to call us all sorts of names especially if we did something stupid. Most of these names were quite endearing e.g. clown, gome, mugadawn, gobaloon, eegit. There was one word that we were all a bit wary of and that was the word 'fecker' and if preceded by 'little' it was a warning that you had really upset him. Erin and Conor may remember this word as they invoked his anger when they picked the only apple from his fledgling tree, which he had been nurturing for years.

He rarely if ever hit us. The only time I got a clout from him was when I killed a swallow with my catapult. It was just a simple slap but it felt like a dagger to the heart! I should add that the leather I used to make the tongue of my catapult was made from his 300 pound, leather, riding boots!

When I was growing up in Ireland there were many occasions when I needed some money. My mum always referred me to my dad on those occasions because he was a much tougher negotiator. My dad never immediately handed over any money without some sort of interrogation. He would say 'how much do you want and I would say 'a pound'. Then he would say 'that's an awful lot of money'. Then he would go through this diatribe: 'when I was your age, I would walk the streets of Dublin with a farthing in my pocket, for months at a time, thinking I was a very rich man, and now you want a pound.' 'Do you know how many farthings there are in a pound?' I eventually did do the calculation-960!! Farthings were still in circulation when I was growing up in Ireland in the 1940s!

I've already told you my bike story so I won't repeat that one but I do have a smoking story. I was friends with the Buggys who lived further up Clonard road near Nicky Kelly's sweetshop. I remember the Buggy's uncle Ned was visiting and he gave Martin and me sixpence each. You could buy a 5 pack of Woodbines for six pence in those days. So Martin and I went to Nicky Kelly's shop and bought a five pack of Woodbines each. I remember they came in a tidy green package. Nicky asked me who they were for and I said my dad! Of course he knew that Mick would never smoke a Woodbine cigarette. I remember it was a very rainy day so we went into the shed and lit up.

Young Ned Buggy, Martin's brother, ran into the shed and saw us smoking and then charged out and announced to his Mum: 'Mammy, mammy Martin and Brendan are smoking in the shed'. Mrs. Buggy lit on us like a banshee and scared the life out of us. I was dispatched to Beechville promptly only to be greeted by Mick who said: 'I hear you've taken up smoking'. He said: 'let me see if you know how to smoke properly?' So he asked me to light up and then told me to inhale deeply, and then told me I wasn't doing it right and that I needed to inhale really deeply. By the time I was finished that cigarette I was as green as the package they came in and never wanted to see another cigarette again. Ten years or so later I did take up smoking and ten years later again, I quit completely after seeing what a smoker's lung looked like during a chest operation. Mick was a heavy smoker himself at one time but finally cut back dramatically to 3 cigarettes a day and I've never seen anyone enjoy those few 'fags' every day, more than he did. He finally quit altogether when he was about 70 years old.

Mick was quite a patient man within limits. I remember a distant relative used to visit us from a neighboring county, from time to time. He happened to be a banker. In addition to that basic character flaw he didn't know when it was time to go home. As Mick said: 'he would talk the hind leg off a donkey'! The clock would strike 10pm and there would be no sign of him leaving. On one occasion Mick and I found ourselves in an untenable situation. The clock had struck 11pm and he was still there talking. I was half dozing off when I heard a bit of commotion. I looked up and saw Mick lying supine, fully stretched out on the dining room table! And Mick said,' there is no rush now Peter, talk away'. That was the end of it. We never saw him again after that!

Many years ago Mick came to America to visit his sister the nun, who lived in San Antonio. One of my former trainees lived there. So I told Billy that we were coming to San Antonio. Billy very graciously organized dinner for us in a reputable restaurant. It was a very enjoyable occasion. It was a Mexican restaurant and they had Mariachi singers and one of them was a particularly good tenor. The menu was written in Hispanic so it was difficult to know what to order. So we ordered what we thought was a reasonable meal and my friend endorsed it. When the meal was over, Mick leaned over and said in a loud, unrestrained voice:' that was easily the worst piece of meat that I have ever tasted in my life'. He had just sampled some goat meat. I don't think he will ever try it again but he will probably remember the Hispanic name for goat-CABRA. My friend Billy was mortified! Mick was a meat inspector for the town of Wexford for about 50 years so he knew a lot about the quality of meat and was never afraid to give his opinion on that subject! You would rarely see goat on the menu in an Irish restaurant!

Mick had some really interesting ideas about banking and insurance, but a lot of his decisions about these issues made sense in retrospect. He rented Beechville for about 25 years and it came with 15 acres of land. The rent on that property was fixed at not much more than 150 pounds per year. That made a lot more sense than paying for a mortgage, with high interest rates during those years.

I thought it was very courageous of him to build his own house when he was in his 60s. We don't know where he got the plans from but he and a few of his friends built that house at the lowest cost imaginable. Fifty years later that house is still pretty solid and beautifully landscaped. I remember getting a call from my mother about 10 years ago during the Celtic Tiger era and she informed me that the house was valued at 1million euro!! Of course then the crash came in 2008 and reality struck. The Banks proved their arrogance and incompetence one more time and of course housing prices were grossly inflated at the time. There are graveyards of abandoned houses all over Ireland, even to this day. Mick was right all along about the banks!! Not one banker went to jail. They were the biggest crooks of all.

CHAPTER 9

Motherhood and the Flag

Patricia Teresa Finucane was born on November 17, 1918. It was a time of jubilation as the Great War had just ended the previous week. She was born in a nursing home in 89 lower Baggot Street in Dublin. Her parents were John and Mary Francis Rutledge. She was the eldest of 4 children, three boys Dermot, Tony, Jack and herself. It would be unfair to say she was born with a silver spoon in her mouth but let's just say that she was, and still is, special. She spent her early years in Dublin, apart from a brief period of schooling in the Ursuline convent in Chester, Cheshire, where she boarded for one year. She was later raised by her three spinster aunts and lived with them on Raymond Terrace on the South Circular Road near Leonard's Corner in Dublin. She was a good student and did well in her Leaving Certificate and learned book keeping in a school on George's Street where her auntie Bridie was a teacher.

The family moved to Wexford when she was 18 or 19 years of age. Her father John Rutledge was hired by Mr. Phil Pierce to be the Chief Engineer of Pierce's Foundry, a large manufacturer of Agricultural Equipment in Ireland at the time. Patricia also worked there and was Phil Pierce's secretary. That was about 1936 and it was in Wexford that she met Mick Finucane and they were married on July 30, 1939 in Bray, County Wicklow.

Patricia Finucane has been in Wexford since about 1936. In round numbers that is about 80 years. I will provide more details of her pedigree in a later chapter.

Despite the fact that our father was essentially a 'meat and potatoes' man, Patricia was an amazing, gourmet cook. She made the most wonderful potato cakes. Rice pudding was another favorite of mine. It was just delicious with slightly brown skin on the outside and I think she used brown sugar and milk as well. She makes wonderful 'pavlovas' too and meringues with whipped cream. She taught me how to make a 'pavlova' recently!!I loved her porridge too and her tea was the best I've ever tasted. When I was in boarding school the food there was awful and when I came home the food was just amazing.

Patricia was very dress conscious and always seemed to know what to wear on any occasion. Even to this day her wardrobe is amazing. She always stood out on special occasions such as weddings and funerals.

Now, life growing up in Beechville wasn't always a bed of roses. My Mum was quite a hard taskmaster. One of the things I didn't like was the 'hand me down' system. My sister Ann was about 18 months older than me, so I always got her 'hand me downs'. For example Ann had a beautiful camel colored coat and when she grew out of it, it became mine. It was a lovely coat but it buttoned on the wrong side. I was very sensitive about stuff like that even though I was only 5 or 6. My Mum said 'no one will notice that', well of course they did. Kids are incredibly smart at noticing differences like that so instead of wearing the coat I would leave it someplace hoping that someone would steal it.

One of the things I always remember about growing up was that I was surrounded by girls. My Dad was at work most of the daylight hours so when I came home from school I was surrounded by girls. I remember when my sister Noeleen was born we went to visit her in a nursing home near where the Stones used to live up there near St. John's Road. Granny was home at the time and when we visited our Mum, Granny gave each of us an angel doll to carry in to surprise our Mum. I wasn't too enamored with the idea but was a bit scared of my Granny so I went along with it, rationalizing that no one would see me here. Well, just as we turned the corner to enter my mother's room, I spotted two of my friends from school-Jimmy and Peter Monaghan. They said 'We didn't know you collected dolls' and every time they met me after that they would say 'how many dolls do you have now?' How embarrassing!!

I never realized what a connection I had with Bray until much later on in life when I put all the pieces together. When I was about 10 or so, although I was a good student I was quite rough around the edges and was always involved in scrapes and getting into trouble with my friends, so to polish me up a bit my parents sent me away to boarding school. It was a 'rite of passage' for families that could afford it. I didn't see it that way at all. To me it was like going to prison. I was dreading the idea of separation from the family. Mum drove me from Wexford to Bray. It was quite a long drive in those days and I was very fretful. We had lunch in the Royal Hotel in Bray and afterwards we climbed Bray Head. I remember asking her if I could see our house from Bray Head. Without hesitation she looked me straight in the eye and said 'On a clear day you might see it'. I was comforted by that answer. That first night in school was the worst I had ever felt. I felt so lonely and abandoned and when I saw the porridge that big Brother Ambrose served I was ready to puke onto my plate. I hated that school for about a month but with time I made friends and started playing rugby and after about three months I told my parents I didn't ever want to come home!

One of the great memories I have of my mother and boarding school was when I was a junior, equivalent to grade 9. Sports Day was held every spring and my Mum always came to visit me on Sports Day. To everyone's surprise I won the 100 yard dash. Even better still my mum won the Mother's race that same day. She left them all standing. That was a special moment in our lives together! My mum took the following picture capturing the start of the Junior 100 yard dash in 1957. My only regret is that I didn't have a photo of the Mother's race.

100 yard dash, PCB, 1957

Another great day I remember was Graduation Day from UCD when I was awarded my degree. My Dad really was not keen to travel to Dublin and some members of the family were not happy with that decision. However I was not bothered by it and gave my dad full permission to miss that event. Mum, Jean and I had a great time (see photo). It was a very big moment for our family and we celebrated all day and Mum and Jean were very stylishly dressed. Graduation Day was in July 1967 and took place at Earlsfort Terrace. I vaguely remember we ended up in Dalky or Killiney that afternoon.

Graduation UCD, July 1967

Seven years of Medical School wasn't a bed of roses for everybody. The expense of it was quite a big sacrifice for the family and not fully appreciated by me at the time. In those days students did not have much responsibility until the day they graduated so we lived the 'lives of Reilly'. We spent way too much time in the pubs on Lower Leeson Street. Hartigan's was one of the favorites of many medical students as was Kirwan House. The other pub in that area was O'Dwyers. One of our distinguished professors 'The Earl Mc Carthy' spent a lot of time in O'Dwyers. It was not unusual to start the week in one of those Houses when the pubs opened at 10AM. Sometimes it's hard to believe how we ever graduated.

I was fortunate to meet a cousin of mine, Eric Finucane, when I was in Dublin. Eric was my third cousin from Kerry. He was a building contractor and lived in Bray. He was a very generous person and single, and seemed to enjoy spending time with us students. He and I became good friends. He gave me more information about my father's side of the family than anyone else and it was Eric who introduced me to my cousin Conor Finucane from Kerry.

I remember one occasion when Eric visited me in Wexford and I was in my usual impecunious state and my request for funding from my parents was firmly denied. That was when my cousin always came to the rescue. We enjoyed several pints and had a nice meal in Rosslare and it was mid-summer. By the time the evening was over it was beginning to get bright again and therefore time for us to come home and lie down for a while. Prior to entering the house I decided to 'water the flowers'. During this process Eric warned me that he saw the curtain moving. I told him that he was hallucinating and nobody would be awake at this time. Well I was totally wrong about that. When we entered the house I was assailed by a very angry lady who released a torrent of abuse on me and clouted me around the head several times. I was quite stunned to start with so I didn't react much to what was happening. Eric was a bystander in all this and wasn't sure what to do except 'say nothing'. My mother broke the ice by offering Eric a cup of tea and he kindly accepted that offer. It was about 5.30 AM at this point. Things had calmed down considerably and we were quietly drinking our tea, when I noticed that my mother was doing her best to stifle obvious laughter. Then I realized what Mum was laughing at. Eric, in the process of drinking his tea, completely missed his mouth and poured the tea in a steady stream on to his lap. He then placed the empty cup on the saucer and continued talking as if nothing had happened. My Mum and I were paralyzed with uncontrollable laughter. We eventually retired to get some sleep.

The jollity of the previous evening was soon forgotten later that day when I dared to resurface. I received a very stern lecture as my mum pointed out to me that 'there was more to being a doctor than passing your exams' and of course she was totally right about this. Relationships were very strained for a long time after that incident. I remember I found a summer job in San Antonio, Texas in 1966 and before I left for America the prodigal son returned to bid farewell to the family and apologize for my bad behavior.

The following year, I worked in Ardkeen Hospital for a year and then I spent 4 years in Liverpool and from there went to North American where I remained for the rest of my life with the exception of multiple visits 'home'

One of the very special moments I shared with my mother and other family members was a visit to Bargy Castle which is a 12th century Norman Fortress near Tomhaggard, County Wexford. I was living in Atlanta at the time and was back in the Old Country visiting family. We had heard that the castle was bought by a retired military man from Britain and that they had converted the castle into a hotel and restaurant. We made a reservation for dinner there one summer's evening in the late 1970s. We had the most wonderful meal there and the ambience was enchanting. We were one of their first customers, so there were very few people there. We were treated like royalty. At the end of the meal the host said he had a little surprise for us so he disappeared for a while and returned (from the wine cellar) with a very old bottle of vintage port. It was the most delicious tasting port I've ever had. I subsequently learned that the owner of the castle was Sir Eric de Burg who was Chris de Burg's maternal grandfather. Our host that evening was Chris de Burg's father! We had one additional big surprise, our host casually mentioned that his son, Chris de Burg was there that evening. So we had the pleasure of meeting one of our idols at that time and he signed the sleeve of his album entitled 'Spanish Train and other Stories. 'Patricia the Stripper' is a particular favorite of ours on that album and we love to tease our mum about that song and we plan to air it on her 100th birthday. I still have that signed album! We were fans of Chris de Burg before we went to Bargy Castle, but after that experience we are fans for life!

My Mum played a major role in my life. I remember the first watch I ever got was a Tissot that she got for me for my birthday. I remember she tried to stimulate my interest in music. She brought me to see Ronnie Rinaldo who played the harmonica and I started playing the harmonica then. I remember she bought me a Sony transistor radio when transistors first became popular. I remember she wakened me up to tell me when the Russians launched Sputnik in 1957 and when Yuri Gagarin became the first man in space in 1961. She was always up-to-date with the latest news even when she lost her vision and her hearing. She has a great sense of humor and still has in her 100th year. She is very stylish in her dress and stands out in a crowd. She recently broke her hip and had a hip re-placement in the hospital I used to work in 50 years ago. She survived that procedure and was back on her feet within 6 months. This was a great test of her metal. We are all looking forward to celebrating her 100th birthday in November 2018.

CHAPTER 10

The 50ᵗʰ Wedding Anniversary Celebration

We celebrated our parents' 50ᵗʰ wedding anniversary on July 31ˢᵗ 1989. This was the first real family gathering that we had ever had, other than weddings. My sister Ann organized the event. It turned out to be a glorious day but in the event of bad weather we had a marquee set up on the back lawn in Roxboro. I remember my father was a very reluctant participant in this event. He was in his 80s at this stage and couldn't stand the idea of socializing. We were hoping that he would make an appearance. I remember getting him a bow tie with flashing lights which he proudly wore at the event. This was really the last big event that we as a family were all together and there are some fabulous photographs to share with you.

L to R, Noeleen, Ann., Patricia and Jean

This was a great photo of all the girls in the Wexford Finucane family as we celebrated that special day on July 31st, 1989. Many of our parents' friends were there also. Brendan Corish, former leader of the Labor party in Ireland was there with his wife Phyllis. Murt Joyce and his wife Eileen were there. Ina Rossiter was there. Our very good friends, Mike and Chris Murphy were there with their boys Brendan and Ryan from Atlanta. Also accompanying them was their friend Karen. Desmond Neill my mother's first cousin was there from Singapore. My sons Mickey and Conor and daughter Erin were also there. The Mc Donald family from Bunclody, were there, including Donal and his mother and Zoe, Mark, Gavin and Vicky. The Evans family from Wales, were also there, namely Andy, Noeleen, Tim and Rachel. My namesake, Dr.Brendan Finucane from Kerry and his wife Joe were there. The Rutledges from Dublin were there in force as well. Also our cousins Brian and Kevin Rutledge from Dublin were present.

We had a lovely meal in the marquee. Speeches were made and we served champagne and we unrolled a gift from the family which was a beautiful carpet. It was a great event and we had lots of fun and shared many stories about times past. We were all delighted that Desmond was present for this event. He came a long way to be with us for this special anniversary. My wife Donna was unable to attend because we had just moved from Atlanta to Edmonton. This was a major cross road in my life also as I was changing jobs and countries! Mickey was 18 at that time and was also at a major cross road in his life. Shortly after this event Mickey joined the British Army and within a year or so was in action in the 1st Gulf War!

Following is a photograph of my father giving his speech.

He described being married for 50 years as being, 'like a very long day.' Also in the picture from L to R, are: Caroline, Jean, Virginia, Tim, Patricia, Kevin, Erin Vicky, Dad and Letty Traynor.

In summary the 50th wedding anniversary celebration was a huge success and most of the credit should go to my sister Ann who put a lot of work into it.

CHAPTER 11

Tracing the Kerry Finucanes

Finucane Family Crest

The Finucanes have been in Ireland for at least 400 years. According to Ancestry there was a Morgan Finucane living in County Clare as early as 1574. Mathias Finucane, supposedly a decendant of Morgan's was appointed King's Counsel (KC) in 1784 and Justice for the Common Pleas in 1794 and lived in Ennistymon House at that time. His son Andrew was granted a coat of arms in 1815 and that is most likely the origin of the Finucane Family Crest. In addition to County Clare a number of Finucane families have lived in the North Kerry region for at least 200 years and still do.

My father was a Kerryman, born on September 4th 1908 in Tarbert. He was the youngest of a large family. How large, was not that easy to find out. Our original estimate was that there were about 8 children in the family. He being the youngest did not remember very much about some of his siblings because they had already left by the time he reached the age of reason. We did meet his oldest sibling named Tommy (02/01/1894) who was about 15 years older than my Dad. Tommy stayed in Tarbert and farmed there until he died in 1976 at age 81. Tommy was revered by my father.

We also met the second oldest member of that family and her name was Margaret (07/08/1896) but was always know as Virgie by my Dad. Margaret was born in 1896. She had a very interesting career. She left Ireland at age 14 to become a nun in America. She left from Cobh with a number of other young girls from Kerry including her first cousin whose surname was Collins. My aunt Virgie was professed as a nun in Many, Louisana, USA in 1913. Her religious name was Sr.Finian. She spent the rest of her life either teaching or as a Principle in convents in the United States. Sr.Finian returned to Ireland twice in her lifetime. The first time she returned was in July of 1939 to attend my parents' wedding. She returned to America about a month before WW2 began. She returned one more time to visit family in the 1950s. I did get to know her quite well. She was stationed in San Antonio, Texas for most of her life. When I was a medical student in Ireland I applied for an externship in San Antonio and I spent the summer of 1966 working in Santa Rosa Medical Center and during my time there I visited my aunt a number of times. She was a very pleasant lady and had beautiful handwriting. I brought my Dad on a special trip to see his sister in 1985. He really enjoyed that visit to her (see photo). When my aunt left Ireland in 1910 there were 16 or 18 young girls on the boat with her. She mentioned that one of the girls died on the passage to America. She and her cousin Sr.Sienna Collins from that original group lived the the longest. My aunt died in Texas in August 1988. She was 92 years old.

Sr. Sienna Collins, Pat, Mick and Sr. Finian (Margaret)

The next child born in my father's family was Mary Finucane (27/10/1897) who according to the 1901 census was 3 years old when that census took place. I have not been able to trace what happened to Mary but I think she may have also become a nun and rumour suggested that she was in a convent in San Francisco.

The next child to be born in that family was Annie (06/07/1899). She married John Foran and died in childbirth on 23/01/1930. She had three children. Annie Foran was the surviving child of that tragedy and later in life married Johnny Bambury. I recently met Marian Stokes in Hampshire and she is a daughter of Johnny and Annie Bambury, my Aunt Annie's grandaughter.

There was another child born named Augustin ? early 1900 but I could find no paperwork other than the 1901 census. I'm assuming that that child died shortly after birth and definitely before her first year. The next child was Ellen Finucane (26/11/1900). I have not been able to trace Ellen Finucane yet. I think she may have married! And we could not trace her because we did not know her married name.

The next child born was Patrick Finucane (15/09/1902). Patrick went to America for a short while and then came back and went to England and I believe worked for the Metropolitan Police (? detective). He lived in Hanwell, London and died in December of 1989. He was married to Susan and had two sons.

After Patrick there was John (Jack) Finucane(14/09/1904). I met Jack and his wife Nellie Dowling. Jack died on 22/04/1992. They had a large family also (9 children). I have met a number of my uncle Jack's children. I recently met Thomas Finucane, Jack's son and Carmel (Thomas's) his daughter.

The next child in my father's family was Danny Finucane (28/02/1907). My father talked a lot about Danny and what happened to him still remains a mystery. There were lots of rumors. I was able to trace him to America with exact details of what ship he left on (Baltic) and when and where. He arrived in New York on 21/06/1926. He filed a petition for citizenship and I was able to obtain his SSN. But I was unable to get any other information. My father maintained that he was a semi-professional boxer and the mob went after him for throwing a fight. Another story was that he died on the bus home after a fight. The third story I heard was that the mob tied him onto the railway tracks and both legs were amputated, but I do not have one iota of evidence that any of these stories are remotely true.

According to my calculations there were 10 children in my father's family. However there is still a bit of confusion about how many there were. I checked the baptismal records in the catholic church in Tarbert and that is where I got the date of birth (DOB) information. In the 1901 census there was a 3 year old female daughter named Rose. That name did not appear in the 1911 census. But there was a 12 year old daughter named Mary. So I am wondering if Rose and Mary are the same person.According to the DOB data I have, Mary was born on 27/10/1897. So in the 1901 census Rose was 3 but would have been 4 in October. So if Rose and Mary are the same person, Mary would have been 3 in the 1901 census. However in the 1911 census Mary is aged 12. So I think there is a good case for Mary and Rose being the same person. Also there was no Rose in the baptismal information I obtained in the church in Tarbert. So my conclusion is that my father had 9 siblings. There is one other interesting fact that I observed that my father, his brothers Jack and Patrick, were all 87 years old when they died!

My grandfather on the Finucane side was Thomas Finucane and he was born on February 13, 1869 and he was born in Kilcolgan. He was one of 7 children, 5 of whom were girls. Thomas married Annie Mullins and they lived in Pyremount in Carhoona, Tarbert. The marriage took place on February 25, 1894 in Tarbert (I have a copy of the marriage certificate). The interesting thing about my grandfather's generation was that 3 Finucanes in that generation married 3 O'Connors ! Patrick Finucane married Nora O'Connor, Jim Finucane (Eric's father) married Molly O'Connor and Annie Finucane married Jack O'Connor. Rumour also suggests that they all got married on the same day. However I cannot verify that fact. Although I never met my Finucane grandfather, simply because he died many years before I was born. He died on October 7th 1930 in Pyremont and he was just 61 years of age. The death certificate indicated that he died of 'the pains' and there was some mention of rheumatism. He was pronounced by his oldest son Thomas. He most likely died from a heart attack. It was a tough year for the family as they lost their father and one of their sisters (Annie) in that same year.

Although I am not finished tracing the genealogy of the Finucanes in our family just yet we have already accounted for 5 generations of Finucanes if you include my generation's children and grandchildren. I joined Wikitree a few years back. It is an excellent site and it is free but you must register. I also joined Ancestry a number of years ago and did a lot of the basic research on the family using that site. That was not a free site but it did allow me to do some good research and although I no longer subscribe to Ancestry I am still registered with them and they allow me access to my family tree and they allow me to add more information to my family tree any time I want. Wikitree is probably the best site for family members interested in the genealogy of our family. You can get permission to access the information I am giving you here. It is very cumbersome to lay out all that information in one page. You would need a huge sheet of paper to do that, but it is really easy to go on line and look at the information nicely tabulated.

There is a restriction on publishing the URLs of these various websites in this publication but all you have to do is 'google' any of these sites and you will get immediate access. However some of them charge!

So let me now tackle the 6th generation of my Finucane Family Tree. My great grandfather's name was Patsy Finucane. He was born in Kilcolgan in 1839 and he died in 1916. He bought some property called The Pottery. He was married to Margaret McEvoy who was born in Ralapane, County Kerry in 1851 and she died on February 13, 1917. I remember my father talking about Patsy and how tall he was. My Dad said that he could jump from one pier of Pyremount to another and that he was 6 ½ feet tall.

The next generation of Finucanes, (7), was named Thomas and he was born in 1818 in Ardmore and was married to a lady named Mary Quinn. The further back we go the less concrete information we have, but this seems to be accurate information based on the oral history handed down by the family and verified by me on Ancestry. They were Patsy's parents and I have no other information on how many children they had.

The next generation (8) of Finucanes was named John Finucane and he was born in 1770 in Ardmore and died in 1843 in Ardmore. He was married to Kate Lynch. Once again the data I have to support this information comes from an oral history handed down by the family with further verification from Ancestry.

Who was John Finucane's father? The information I obtained from the internet was that Mathias Finucane (1736-1814) had a son named John. Mathias Finucane was a well educated (Trinity College Law) man and married Ann O' Brien, daughter of Edward O'Brien of Ennistymon House which was originally Ennistymon Castle. Ann O'Brien was related to the Earls of Thomond. Mathias Finucane and O'Brien were divorced in 1793. The Right Honorable Mathias Finucane then moved to Lifford House. I don't have good data to support the claim that Mathias Finucane was John Finucane's father but the genealogy data I have up to that time is very reliable. In other words we can reliably say that our branch of the Finucane family have been in Ireland for at least 8 generations and a number of them are buried in Lisnaughton and Kilnaughton cemetaries in North Kerry near Tarbert. My father intimated to me many times that the Finucanes were Hugenots that left France in the middle ages because of religious persecution.

Many Finucanes emigrated to the New World and achieved fame and fortune. But one member of the Finucane clan deserves special mention and that is Brendan Eamon Finucane DSO DFC & 2BARS otherwise known as 'Spitfire Paddy'. He joined the RAF at the minimum eligible age of 18 and in a few years became one of the most decorated pilots in World War 2. He became the youngest Wing Commander in RAF history and is credited with as many as 32 kills during his short career in the RAF. He was shot down over the English Channel on July 15, 1942 at age 21 and was forced to ditch off the coast of France (Le Toquet) and was never found and presumably drowned. Even though Ireland was neutral during WW 2 many Irishmen, like Brendan Finucane, gave their lives to protect us from the rise of Fascism and Nazism in Europe.

I have very little information on the Mullins family yet. My grandfather married Annie Mullins. The marriage certificate indicates that her family owned or rented Pyremount. Apparently Annie Mullins's sister was a midwife and lived with the Finucanes in Pyremount, so she probably delivered many of the children in that family. Rumour has it that Annie Finucane (nee Mullins) went to America for some time and worked in New York but I have no specifics. I have quite a bit of work to do on the Mullins side of the family!

CHAPTER 12

Genealogy of the Dublin Rutledges

Rutledge Family Crest

Based on information I obtained from Ancestry and other sources, the Rutledge name, sometimes spelled Routledge, was originally found around the English and Scottish borders between Carlisle and Berwick. The first actual record of the name Rutledge was found in

Cumberland in the 16th century. There is a place called Routledge Burn in Cumberland, England today.

A significant number of Rutledge families moved to Northern Ireland during the Ulster Plantation. Today the Rutledge name is found in many countries around the world but mainly in the UK, Ireland, USA and Canada. In 1911, 182 Rutledge families lived in Ontario, Canada. So let me now give you some information about my immediate Rutledge ancestors.

I have provided quite a bit of information about my mother Patricia Teresa Finucane (nee Rutledge). My mother had three siblings, all boys, Dermot, Jack and Tony and she was the eldest child. Their parents were John Rutledge and Mary Francis Muriel Howard. John Rutledge was from Dublin and MFM Howard was from the North of Ireland originally (Dungannon, County Tyrone). My grandparents met in a munitions factory in Rathmines in Dublin where my grandfather worked as the Works Manager. Two of the Howards sisters worked in this munitions factory during WW1 run by Sir Howard Grubb and one of them was my grandmother. Sir Howard moved his business to St. Albans shortly after my grandparents met. My grandparents were married on March 2nd 1918 and rumor has it that as this was a mixed marriage (catholic/protestant) they could not be married on the altar so they were married in the Presbytery and the church was St. Kevins on Harrington Street in Dublin.

Let me now trace the Rutledges starting with my grandfather John who was born in 1881. He had 7 siblings many of whom I met. His oldest sibling was Robert, born in 1880, then there was John born in 1881, followed by Edward in 1883, then Andrew in 1885, Julia in 1887, Rose in 1890, Joseph in 1892 and Brigid in 1893. Their parents were Andrew Rutledge (b.1849) and Rebecca Walsh (b.1855) and they married in the church of St.Nicholas of Myra on 25/08/1878. I can go back one step further to Robert Rutledge, my great, great grandfather. He was born in 1821 and was married to Elizabeth Carroll. Robert was a slater and built Raymond Street and Love Lane. He died on November 15, 1906.

So altogether we have at least 7 generations of Rutledges from Dublin that we can trace back as far the early 1800s.The Rutledges owned several properties in the South side of Dublin and the family lived for many years in 32 Raymond Terrace, South Circular Road(SCR). There is a terrace near SCR name Rutledge Terrace which was owned by the Rutledge family.

My grandfather was a very bright man by all accounts and was very eligible for a college education but unfortunately that did not happen. He attended the Christian Brother's School at Synge Street in Dublin. I already mentioned that he worked as Works Manager for Sir Howard Grubb in the munitions factory in Rathmines. He also was the chief engineer for Pierce's Foundry in Wexford in the 1930s. He worked for Presteel in Oxford after WW2. My mother tells the story that he was called to fix a broken telescope in Birr County Offaly. This was no ordinary telescope. According to Wikipedia, this was the world's largest telescope until 1917. It was named 'The Leviathon of Parsonstown' and was built by Sir William Parsons, the 3rd Earl of Rosse, in Birr Castle in 1845. The telescope was six feet in height and had a huge reflecting mirror and had an aperture of 72 inches. It remained functional until about 1890. There was renewed interest in the telescope after Patrick Moore, a well known astronomer and TV personality from England encouraged new interest in this historical masterpiece in 1970. A new reflecting mirror was installed in 1999 and by all accounts the telescope is working again in modern times and for tourists to Ireland, it would be well worth a vist to see this treasure.

I did meet my grandfather but have no real memory of him as I was too young. He died in Oxford at age 64 from a heart attack in 1945. The family moved to Wexford around 1936 and my mother has been there ever since. This is a photograph of my grandfather (left) looking out the window of their home at 45 Fernhill Road, Cowley, Oxford. I'm not sure of the year but estimate it to be early to mid 1940s and I believe that the person on the right is Tony Rutledge his son.

I think you might be interested to know that Edward Rutledge from South Carolina was the youngest signee of the Declaration of Independence of the United States, at age 26. His older brother John achieved even greater notoriety. John was born in Charleston, South Carolina in 1739. His father was a medical doctor. John had a great interest in law from a very early age. He was educated at Middle Temple in London, England and became one of the most prominent lawyers in Charleston. He became the 31st Governor of South Carolina in 1779. He was appointed Associate Justice to the Supreme Court of the United States by George Washington in 1790. He also served as a delegate to the Stamp Act Congress which vigorously opposed taxes imposed on the 13 Colonies by the British Parliament.

Let's now trace the Howard family. My grandmother Rutledge was a Howard. Mary Francis Muriel Howard was one of 7 children born to Samuel Howard who married Maud Hinds in 1890. Samuel was a presbyterian from County Tyrone and he practiced as a solicitor. Maud Hinds was from County Offaly and she was a patron of the Church of Ireland. They were married in 1890 and they had 7 children but I don't know the order of their births. According to the 1911 Irish census William(Edward) Howard was 20 years old, Arthur was 19, Grace was 18. Then there were 4 other children, among them Monica, who died at a young age. Then there was auntie Vick, Mary Francis Muriel and Patricia, none of whom appeared in the 1911 census because they were all away at boarding school in England. The Howards lived in Dublin

South but I'm not sure when they moved there but they were in Dublin in 1901 when the census was taken.

According to my mother one of the Howard boys played rugby for Ireland. I have not been able to verify that but I hope to follow-up on that soon. Grace Constance Howard otherwise known as auntie Gee was married to James Scott Neill who worked for the foreign service. He was a Trinity graduate in Law and spent most of his life in the South Sea islands, initially in Fiji and eventually in Tonga. He wrote a very interesting book about his experiences in Tonga during Queen Salote's reign. The title of the book was : Ten Years in Tonga. He was asked to adjudicate a case involving larceny by a member of the royal family and that is what brought him to Tonga. He was highly respected by Queen Salote and was invited to be her guardian when she came to England for the Queen's coronation in 1953. Auntie Gee had one child, James Desmond Howard Neill. She was incredibly lonely because she lived so far away. I traced her travels on ship manifests from Belfast to Fiji which she did on her own when she was a young woman. It would take her ages to get from Fiji to Belfast but she was so lonely she was willing to make that sacrifice so that she could go home to see her mother. To give you an idea of her travels starting in Belfast, she would board a ship in Belfast taking her to St.John, New Brunswick on the east coast of Canada and then take a train across Canada from New Brunswick to Vancouver, British Columbia and then board a ship there that would take her to Fiji. It would take her the best part of a month to get to Fiji from Belfast. She wrote to her mother one time saying 'I'm very important here but I would rather be a worm at home'! Auntie Gee died at quite a young age of 55. Samuel Howard died in 1962 and I was able to go back one more generation from Samuel to his father who was also Samuel Howard and he was married and had four children. He died in 1916. So we can trace back as far as 7 generations in the Howard family also.

Mary Francis Muriel Howard, my grandmother was quite a character and although I knew only one of four of my grandparents as the other 3 died either before I was born or when I was very young but grandmother

Rutledge made up for what I missed with the other three. She had a very strong personality and you would never want to cross her! On each grandchild's birthday we would receive a beautifully written card from Granny Rutledge with an enclosure of a crisp brand new pound note. That was quite a lot of money in the 40s! She never missed a birthday and the card always arrived on the exact day of your birthday! She was not intimidated by anyone.

I recall a story my mother told me about Granny. Her boys went to Synge Street school in South Dublin run by the Christian Brothers. One of her boys was not doing so well in school so the christian brother decided to humiliate him by bringing his younger brother into the class to show him how to do a math problem. When Granny Rutledge heard about that she charged into the school and demanded to see the brother. When he appeared she slapped him and warned him, never to do that again! Can you imagine anyone daring to tackle the clergy in this way in Ireland in the 1920s?

There was another occasion that I remember well. Granny Rutledge housed a young Irish girl who had come to England to work. This young lady (Teasy) got married and was travelling back to Ireland to see her family there. I was visiting my grandmother at the time and was travelling back with Teasy and her new baby Susan. Granny decided that she would take the train with us part of the way as we were catching the mail boat from Fishguard to Rosslare. The journey was going well until the conductor discovered that we were sitting in the wrong carriage. Granny had put us in the first class carriage. When the conductor continued to threaten us she got up right into his face and pushed him and told him not to come back. So we stayed where we were. When we got to Crewe, where she was getting off, she said: 'watch him now, he's going to report me to the stationmaster, as if I care'.

In 1930 she was awarded a silver cup as the top Hoover sales person in Dublin. I think my mother still has that cup! I've added a photograph of Granny Rutledge below with my mother, Teasy and my sister Jeanne.

**L to R Pat Finucane, Mary Francis Rutledge,
Teasy McCracken and Jean Finucane**

I would be remiss if I did not mention another one of our very distinguished relatives on my mother's side of the family and that is of course Desmond Neill, my mother's first cousin. Desmond was the only child of auntie Gee and James Scott Neill. He went to the Dragon School in Oxford and was a very good friend of John Mortimer the famous author of Rumpole of the Old Bailey whom he had met at the Dragon School. Desmond joined the military during WW2 and was stationed in the far east and when he was demobbed in Singapore in 1945 he decided to stay there. He learned how to speak the dialect of Chinese-Hokkien preferred by immigrants to Singapore. He was awarded an MBE when he was 33 years old for secret negotiations with communists on behalf of Britain in Malaya. He became friends with Lee Kuan Yew and remained so during Lee Kuan Yew's tenure as Prime Minister of Singapore. He was offered a job by Fraser and Neave, a large brewing company in Malaysia, upon retiring from the Malasian Civil Service. He was rapidly promoted and eventually became the CEO of the company. That company thrived under his tenure as CEO. He was a brilliant negotiator. He travelled the world and was a renowned linguist. He was an incredibly generous man and an enthralling raconteur. He published a really interesting book about Singapore entitled 'Elegant Flower'. Sadly he died on May 27, 2017, aged 93. He will not be forgotten by our family for many reasons, not the least of which was his generosity.

Patricia Finucane with James Desmond Neill, 31ˢᵗ July 1989

Recollections, Sayings, Stories and Poems in Honor of Patricia Finucane's 100th Birthday

A s this is a very special occasion, we appealed to all of Patricia's relatives and friends, to write something that they remember about an interaction or happening they experienced with Patricia.

Stories and Sayings from the McDonald Family

When I was a young girl, Granny would sometimes take me on an adventure to the big smoke also known as (a.k.a.) Dublin. Granny always seemed a little racy compared to my friend's grandmothers. She would drive me to Dublin in her trusty red Toyota Starlet wearing her brown leather gloves and an outrageously fashionable outfit with strong shoulder pads. "I'm going a hundred miles an hour," she announced gleefully on one such trip as we sped past the Sugarloaf mountains. My heart would race, and I worried if it was safe for me to be alone with this tearaway woman.

While we were in Dublin, we would shop, go to the horseshow and gallivant about town, but the adventure that sticks with me most is the time she took to me to McDonald's restaurant in Stillorgan. The taste of chicken nuggets and BBQ was something I had never tasted before and going there without my parents felt even more illicit. Granny took delight in seeing my face as I devoured all this new, strange food. These little *Thelma and Louise* getaways of ours always made me feel very grown-up.

A few years ago, it was me who took granny on another little adventure. I took her to Arklow in my trusty Toyota Yaris. I drove cautiously and certainly didn't break the speed limit. We went to the shopping center and browsed TK Maxx for clothes. Given my gran's love of fast food, I thought it was only fitting that we go to the fast food court for lunch. We took a plastic seat, and I went up and got granny a bagel. Just before taking a bite of the bagel, she started to splutter with laughter. I asked her what was so funny. She replied, "I've never had a bagel before."

So dear granny — I know we've shared a lot of really good food together, and your Pavlovas are the stuff of legend, but these little outings and our shared wonder over fast food are memories that I will always hold dear.

Love, Vicky

Granny routinely came on summer holidays to France with the McDonald family. We'd squeeze five people into the back of the Peugeot and spend a few weeks traversing the highways and byways of Normandy and Brittany. We grew up to appreciate great food and local French delicacies were always a feature on these summer trips. As a teenager I was fascinated by Granny's love for live crustaceans, shellfish, snails and just about any unusual edible organ, bird or animal on the menu! One vacation comes to mind when we stopped, *en route* to the ferry port in beautiful Honfleur, Normandy. Endless platters of colorful crustaceans were brought out along with escargot and some other snail like creatures. The chef may have done this deliberately to joke with the Irish tourists but out of one innocent shell appeared a friendly set of tentacles. Granny picked the helpless creature up and sucked down the very "live" contents grinning from ear to ear as she savored the contents. She earned hero status with me that day!

I have noticed as she continues into her late 90's that she still has a hearty appetite. Here's to the 100 year old with the iron stomach! Hopefully I have inherited her adventurous spirit when it comes to food and her strong constitution to accompany that spirit!

Love, Zoe

I recall when I was young Granny and Jeanne being inseparable – the telephone exchange every morning, the latest strategy and trips to Europe for their clothes store Top Drawer and family dinner every single Sunday without fail, which in retrospect demonstrates what a fulcrum of the family Granny has always been. One time when I was at boarding school in Rockwell, Granny accompanied mum for the trip. I recall the smiles and teasing she gave Mum when the principle Fr. Hurley expressed his delight to meet mums sister! Granny has always defied the effects of aging and even then, she looked 20 years younger than she was.

I spent many summer school breaks staying for one or two weeks with Granny and Grandad, helping maintain their property. I was lucky to experience attending some point-to-point horse races where I admired my grandparents network with the horse fraternity Granny made it a special adventure. I'm not sure if it was around that time but Granny acquired the use of a word called "queer'n" and always loved using it as an adjective – like that's "queer'n bad" or that's "queer'n fast" always with a chuckle on her newly found slang word!

Granny, thank you for being the indomitable spirit, who has inspired me on the power of positivity and humor in everyday life.

Love, Mark

One of Pat's great interests in life was going to Auctions, especially when there was antique furniture involved. I remember one particular occasion when she and Jean set off to Mealy's Auction Rooms in Castlecomer. Pat bid for a kitchen dresser and, having purchased, she realized that transporting it home was going to be a problem, but not for long. They loaded the dresser on the roof of the car, a yellow Renault called "The Yellow Banana!" The dresser was held in place with cardboard and tied with ropes and was a great source of amusement to passers-by. What a surprise they got when they arrived home to great applause from family and neighbors who were intrigued by the sight of the travelling dresser.

On my 1st visit to Roxboro, Pat had prepared a delicious meal - she was a brilliant cook. After the main course she told me she had made a special dessert for me and invited me into the kitchen. She opened the oven door and took out a meringue cake. Then she served it and to my surprise it contained a whole block of ice cream. . . . out of the oven!! It was Baked Alaska and she still laughs when she relates this story.

Love, Donal

Sunday Lunches in Roxboro and Drumderry

From as young as I can remember, Sundays have been spent with Granny in Roxboro or Drumderry. The tradition is one to treasure as the food was always amazing- let it be a leg of lamb or roast beef. One thing that Granny always insists on or is fussy about was how the gravy was made- I was trained up in the gravy making duties and it is a skill that hasn't let me down to this very day.

Granny's Gravy:

Once meat is cooked, pour off the fat out of the pan. Let the meat rest on a board.

Add a small teaspoon of flour, a pinch of stock to the pan and heat gently, stirring all the time.

Now add a splash of wine or sherry (or both) and continue stirring. Then add the juices from the resting meat. (She insists that this is where all the flavor is!).

Add a small amount of boiling water and return mixture to heat and reduce to make Granny's gravy.

This is only one of Granny's tricks that she taught me from the kitchen.

Love, Gavin

Recollections from the Dublin Rutledge Family

My longest memory of Patricia (known to my family as Auntie Pat), was being welcomed into a Georgian house in Clonard in 1965 with club orange and biscuits. Then we rode a small horse around an orchard and back of the house in the company of the younger Finucanes. Not a surprise that we always wanted to visit Auntie Pat. Then in 1980 I arrived in Wexford to work as a junior doctor in the hospital. Once more she was to the fore inviting me out to lunch and dinner, introducing me to James Sinnott and others. She was always welcoming interesting and interested and had a phenomenal knowledge of rugby and current affairs. Three years ago, aged 97 she came to visit Christine and I in Kilmore Quay for dinner and when asked what would she like to drink she responded 'whatever you are having, I will have a large one (gin and tonic)'. She is a phenomenal, gracious and hospitable lady. Cheers, Damian Rutledge (nephew).

Stories, Sayings and Poems from the Finucane Family

My Mum has a great sense of humor and always enjoyed a good laugh. I remember one time she appeared to be quite unwell. I'm not sure what was wrong but she was confined to bed for days. I was at a morbid stage in life when I was about eight years old and was always worried that something would happen to my parents. I spent what seemed like hours waiting outside her bedroom worrying about her and after a very prolonged vigil she called me in and told me to get a pen and paper and to write down whatever she said. I thought this was very serious. So she started and spelled it out for me: 'HOOF HEARTED ICE MELTED' Then she said 'read it back quickly out loud. It's very important'. So, I did! When I realized what it said, we both burst out laughing, uncontrollably. So then I knew she probably was going to live at least one more night! That was 70 odd years ago! And she's 100 today!

She had some great sayings, for example, whenever we talked about riches or wealth she would say: 'There are no pockets in a shroud'. Whenever she was talking about someone who was a little bit on the stingy side she would say: 'Ah, that one is so mean you couldn't see her heart on a clean plate'. If you tried to tell Pat a tall story she would say: 'Go tell that to the Marines.' Another favorite of hers was: 'Man proposes God disposes.'

I remember when we were very young she gave us autograph books. It was a trendy thing to do in those days, so I asked her to write something in my autograph book. So she wrote:

Have new Friends

Keep the Old

These the Silver

Those the Gold

Happy 100th Birthday Mum, you are one in a million! Love always, Brendan

One time, I was visiting Wexford and it was quite cold. Granny was really worried about me getting cold, coming from Canada, so she followed me around from room to room with a small electric heater. We were sitting down to eat in the dining room later that evening and Granny set up the heater for me. The next thing I knew, my sweater was on fire!

On that same visit to Wexford, I developed a bit of a chill. Granny knew exactly what I needed on that occasion so she went out and bought me some pig's feet (trotters!) and said 'that'll crown her!'

Happy 100th Birthday Mum, Love, Donna

Sister Angela asked me to draw a picture of Jesus Christ
I did my best but it wasn't quite right

I asked Mum if she would help me please
This she did with the greatest of ease

Sister Angela said she was quite impressed
But sadly it didn't pass the test

Because only my mother knows
Why she drew Jesus with six toes

We flew to Dublin when Sarah was about 16 months old. We agreed to meet Mum and Ann in the Stillorgan Park Hotel. When we arrived, Polly needed to go to the bathroom and Mum said she would go with her. Mum warned Polly that there was a step down which people keep falling on. On the way Mum fell over the step and immediately picked herself up saying to Polly "See I told you people keep falling over that step" and then erupted in roars of laughter.

On that same trip Mum, Polly and I had tickets to see a play in the Abbey Theatre called Boss Grady's Boys. Unfortunately a couple of hours before-hand Sarah wasn't very well and Polly said she wouldn't go. As Mum and I had consumed a couple of large G & T s Ann dropped us off. During the first half of the play Mum was very fidgety (it was a very boring play). At the interval, Mum said to me: "Thank God for that I'm dying to go to the bathroom". We settled down for the second half and about 5 minutes in Mum started to snore very loudly, I nudged her and she woke up with a start and said "I'm awake". She settled down again and within a couple of minutes the same thing happened again. I was trying to stifle my laughter! It was a very boring play!

Happy 100th Birthday Mum, Love always, Peter

Granny is a great conversationalist and is never shy of having a contro-versial opinion, on any topic. Her views on Catholicism and the GAA are particular favorites of mine, and best left undocumented.

Since introducing Lynne to the family Granny has freely shared with me her perceptions on "The North". Lynne passed her initial inspection by Granny and was allowed to sit next to her at dinner! Her role as a great grandmother has not always run smoothly. On one of Archie's first visits to Wexford she was convinced he was reluctant to go to her and stated "He hates me". Adding Seth to the mix was never good for my anxiety levels particularly when he was within toppling distance, of the marvelous porcelain dogs at Roxboro.

Granny and I share a love of most sports but especially Rugby. She is a passionate Leinster and Ireland supporter. She loves to remind me of Leinster's numerous victories over Ulster, and of those odd occasions when Ireland manages to scrape home against Wales!

Congratulations on your 100th Birthday Granny, with love from Mickey, Lynne, Archie and Seth

My Granny has always had interesting things to teach me about life. I remember being in the kitchen with her one day, pretty sure Granny was teaching me how to make soups. She was always an incredible cook. I had just asked what the age gap was between her and Grandad. Granny informed me that Grandad was ten years older than her, which surprised me. She then dropped in this amazing gem of life advice…I had to marry an older man you know, men and women age differently and there was no plastic surgery in my day. It's alright for you Sonya (Saaanya in granny's lovely southern Irish drawl) you can marry a man any age you want and then have the plastic surgery when you need it. So far I've managed to avoid the plastic surgeons scalpel, but I'll keep it in mind Granny, thanks.

Another thing you should know about my Granny, she does love a gin. I remember arriving in Wexford one day, Granny greeted me in the kitchen with a 'will you have a gin!!??' Not being a lover of gin at the time I said no thanks Granny, I don't like gin. Granny, unperturbed by this said 'well sure, have a vodka, I have orange juice and schnapps, I'll make you a furry navel, is that what it's called?'

It's a fuzzy navel Granny, but that works for me and is what it's always been called in my head since!! She's a cracker!

Love you Granny and Happy 100th Birthday!

Sonya

Granny has taught me a lot over the years. The knowledge I think she would most like to bestow on me is a little bit of her fashion sense. There is no doubt in my mind, Granny is a fashionable woman, I distinctly remember her wearing blue nail polish at Niamh's wedding.

One day, my Dad said, he was coming back from Ireland and had a gift for me from Granny. I was surprised and excited, having no idea what it was. After returning from Ireland, Dad came over immediately and he held out his hand. (I had company over). He then passed me...a ball of fabric. After unraveling it, I understood the bizarre handling of this gift. It was a lacy, red thong. If that's not fashion, I don't know what is. It's not every day your Granny picks out a thong for your Dad to give to you!

If I were to offer any suggestion about transferring a gift like that in the future, I might suggest wrapping paper could aid in the delivery.

Love you, Granny and Happy 100th Birthday

Erin

I have many fond memories of visiting Granny and Grandad at the home in Wexford when I was young. The bonfires we would have just beyond the fence and the wild horses that we would see run past in the field beyond from time-to-time. I remember looking up at the horses in the barn in awe, as these majestic beasts shadowed over me. There was a red stallion that they called Big Red that was my favourite. We would get into so much mischief running around with so much land to explore. Erin and I once did something that made Granny very upset - we ate the only apple that ever grew on this tree in the backyard and got a clear sense of the strictness that our dad was raised within his household.

When we came to Rachel's wedding in 2012, I had an opportunity to spend some quality time with Granny again after many years without seeing her. We were in a pub in Wales and I was explaining to her how I had met this girl from Mexico that I was becoming serious with and was showing her pictures of Mary from my phone. I showed her some of her dancing as well as one that I had drawn of Mary. She was so intrigued to hear about Mary and simply said that, "she looks just lovely". Mary had missed the wedding and met up with us after in London and we went on a trip from there. I really wish that Granny and Mary had the opportunity to meet each other in person and the plan was for that to happen at Granny's 100th birthday this year. I know that Mary was really looking forward to the trip and seeing Granny and Ireland for the first time.

The last time I saw Granny, was in 2015 when we came to the UK to watch the World Cup of Rugby. When I walked into the Wexford Manor, Granny was in the corner of the living room, sitting on a chair not 2 feet from the a small tube television The TV looked like it was from the 80's and she was staring into the screen watching a rugby match with the sound blaring. Granny at nearly 97 years old at this time had trouble seeing and hearing much, but nothing was going to stop her from enjoying her rugby and the climbing Irish squad. Anne, Niamh and I had a chuckle over that and then we went out for a nice dinner together and caught up. It had probably been over 20 years since I had been back to the Manor, but not much had changed from my fond childhood memories of the house, yard and time spent with our family in Ireland.

Happy 100th Birthday Granny!

Love, Conor

I especially loved seeing Granny a few years ago when she met Ashley and I and proceeded to take us on a tour of Wexford. She's was dressed up so beautifully and she had lots of friends that she was running into on the street. You could tell she was proud to introduce us. Then we ended up going for lunch and dinner at the same restaurant. Clearly it was her favorite. And you should have seen the size of the bowl of mussels they brought her!

Happy 100th Birthday Granny,

Love, Kevin and Ashley

Recollections from the Canadian Rutledge Family

I always reflect on the time that Grace, Vivian and I went to Wexford to visit our aunt and Ann several years ago. Aunt Pat was so welcoming, loving, kind and so interested to know who we were. She is a gracious host and cooked the most amazing dinners with salmon (bay leaf and wine) and heating raspberries over top of cookie dough ice cream... one of my favourites to date. We talked, walked and enjoyed her garden, while listening to stories of our dad and his family through the years. She made us feel important and part of the family. She also had so many pictures that she shared with us. Ann was also so lovely and took us for a few shopping trips in the area and we stayed at the best B&B with the best Irish breakfast, with horses visible out of our window. Looking so forward to seeing her again and celebrating her 100th birthday!

We love you Auntie Pat and Happy 100th Birthday!

Sheila

In the spring of 2018 I had the opportunity to meet Aunt Pat on a trip to Ireland with my cousin and good friend, Brendan Finucane. Brendan had planned every detail of this trip, for my sake. Amongst many other adventures, we visited Aunt Pat and Anne for lunch. We had never met before, but we had heard so much about each other. We spoke of John (Jack) Rutledge (my father), and many memories she had of him. He passed away 40 years ago at this time. She had an incredible memory at her age of 99 as we reminisced with stories of her childhood and my father. We enjoyed a beautiful lunch that Anne had prepared for us, with the table set so perfect and royal like, and Aunt Pat sitting at the head of the table. She was very respected by her family.

Happy 100th Birthday Aunt Pat

Love, Brendan

Recollections from the Evans Family

Rachel and I have been thinking a lot about Granny…there are so many memories we have. We cannot compile these into one anecdote but wonder if more than a few of us may recognise the familiarity of some of these "one liners"!

- the yellow Renault 21

- the red Toyota Starlet

- the journeys!!

- the Absolut and tonic

- the formidable Sunday lunches

- with veterinary career aspirations (on my part) asked what do you call cows sent off with a bull…"going off to profit"!!!

Wonderful memories we hold very close, we cannot wait for this great occasion!

Happy 100th Birthday Granny!

Love always, Tim and Rachel and Evans Family

Patricia Finucane with her Family, April 2018

POST SCRIPT

This is the first edition of what I hope will become a standard storybook to be read by our descendants for generations to come. It is just amazing what has happened in our world in one hundred years. Can you imagine what it must have been like to live without a telephone, electricity or a car? Can you imagine what it will be like in 2118? Actually it is very likely that some of the people attending Pat Finucane's 100th birthday celebration will actually live to tell that tale and hopefully share those stories in a future edition of this book.

What I tried to capture in this book is what people thought, said, felt and did during the past 100 years, because things are changing so fast this information will be lost unless we write it down. Just look at what *Twitter* has done to language in the space of a couple of decades. People are not communicating like we did even 50 years ago. Can you imagine what it will be like in another 100 years? By then we probably will have colonised Mars! There is a prediction out there, that travel, from New York to Sydney will take 30 minutes within the next 25 years!!

I cannot guarantee the accuracy of some of the stories I shared with you and I'm quite sure some of them have been embellished over the years and are now part of the folklore of our family. It was not my intention to denigrate or ridicule any particular profession, gender, race or creed in the process of writing this book. Hopefully you will appreciate that in true Irish form the writer himself is the recipient of a considerable portion of the ridicule served up.

You can all help me by adding your up-to-date information to the genealogy chapters. So please do not hesitate to share your unique knowledge of your family history with me and I will update the information in future editions of this publication. I would also appreciate it if you notice some inaccuracies, especially in the genealogy chapters, please don't hesitate to point them out to me.

It has been a pleasure working on this project. Thank you all for your contributions and now let us all toast our amazing centenarian Patricia Teresa Rutledge with a traditional Gaelic Blessing:

May the road rise up to meet you
May the wind be always at your back
May the sun shine warm upon your face;
the rains fall soft upon your fields
and until we meet again,
may God hold you in the palm of His hand.

ABOUT THE AUTHOR

Dr.Finucane is originally from Ireland and has a medical degree from University College Dublin. He has lived in North American for the past 46 years and practiced Medicine in universities in both Canada and the United States. He is a medical writer and has published a number of scientific articles in anesthesiology and two text books. His interests include history, amateur writing, travel and sports.

Printed in Great Britain
by Amazon

21547195R00052